Woven with Brown Thread

Edited by Upile Chisala

Published in 2021 by The Centre for the Less Good Idea NPC.
Arts on Main
Unit 13, 264 Fox Street
City and Suburban
Johannesburg
2094
Registration No. 2019/355432/08

Email: lessgoodidea@gmail.com
Website: www.lessgoodidea.com

An anthology as part of the Khala Series 2021 100 Poem Project.
Edited by Upile Chisala
Supported by The Centre for the Less Good Idea NPC.
Graphic design: www.prinsdesign.co.za
Cover Illustration: Neo Phage

ISBN: 978-1-991217-63-9

Supported by:

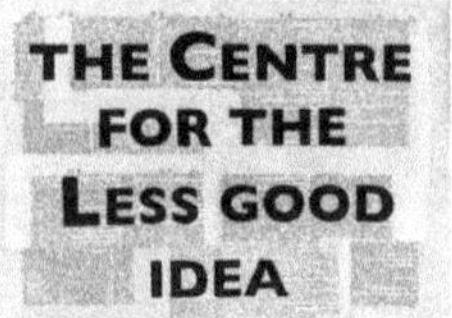

The 100 Poem Project
— *Upile Chisala*

Here are the parts of us that we wove together
with brown thread,

to make a thing of memory,
of sorrow,
of joy,
of forgiveness,
of what is gone
and of what will come after,
of heartache
and
of deep miraculous love.

This is a book in celebration
and in remembrance.

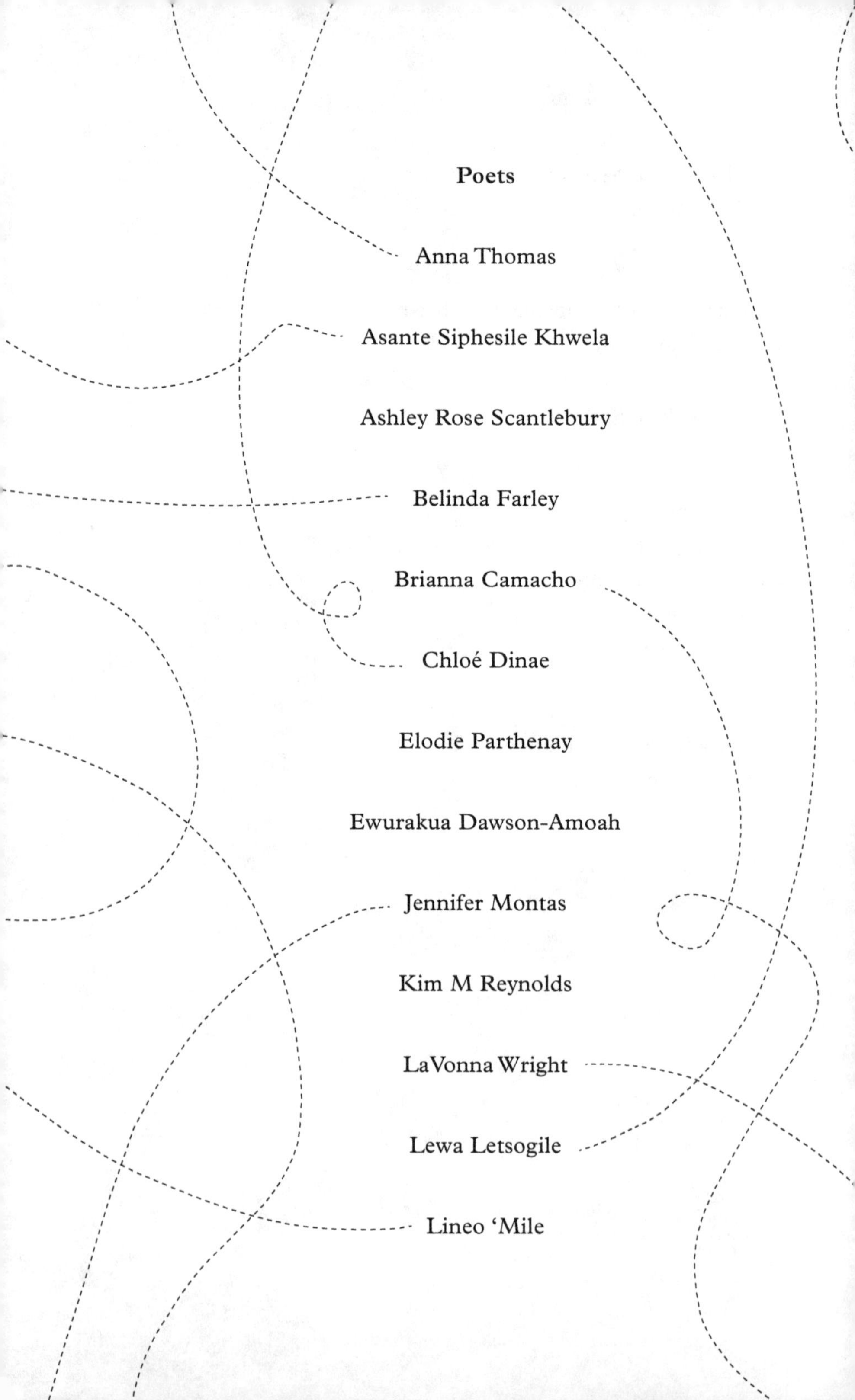

Poets

Anna Thomas

Asante Siphesile Khwela

Ashley Rose Scantlebury

Belinda Farley

Brianna Camacho

Chloé Dinae

Elodie Parthenay

Ewurakua Dawson-Amoah

Jennifer Montas

Kim M Reynolds

LaVonna Wright

Lewa Letsogile

Lineo 'Mile

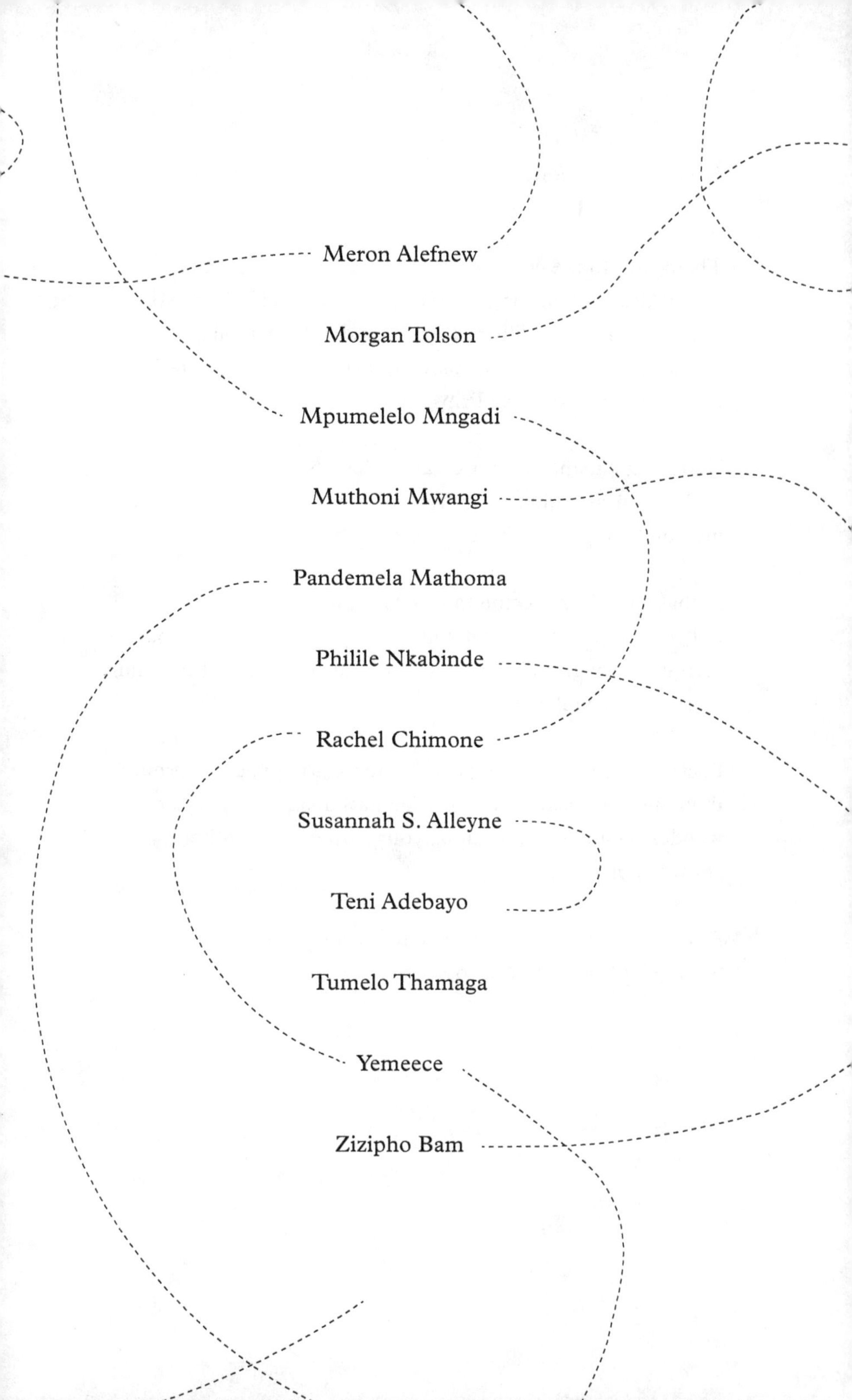

Meron Alefnew

Morgan Tolson

Mpumelelo Mngadi

Muthoni Mwangi

Pandemela Mathoma

Philile Nkabinde

Rachel Chimone

Susannah S. Alleyne

Teni Adebayo

Tumelo Thamaga

Yemeece

Zizipho Bam

Acknowledgements

Thank you to the entire team at The Centre for the Less Good Idea for believing in this project. A special thank you to Bronwyn Lace, William Kentridge, Phala O. Phala, Dimakatso Motholo, Athena Mazarakis, Bongile Lecoge-Zulu, Noah Cohen and Adéle Prins.

Neo Phage, thank you for creating this book's cover with such kindness and thought. You remain the softest and most incredible of people I've ever met.

Lethabo Mailula, I came to you with this idea, and not only did you tell me to go for it you stayed in my corner and have seen me through to its completion. Your friendship is the thing of dreams. Thank you.

Poets of this collection, thank you for sharing your innermost thoughts and feelings with us. You have made this project a wonder. Thank you for telling your stories. This anthology is always yours first.

And to all poets, in this book and beyond, thank you for writing and sharing. Your poems are necessary.

Contents

Introduction

This anthology is the result of deep heart work. Seeing
Woven with Brown Thread come alive is one of my greatest
dreams realized. When I started the Khala Series writing
mentorship program my hope was to sit in a room with
other poets and work through our work. In 2019, every other
Saturday in Johannesburg for weeks Khala Series happened.
We met, we laughed, we held each other, we cried, and
we occasionally wrote. It was such a filling experience to
be among the words and those who live to navigate them.
With 2020, came the pandemic and lockdown and Khala,
like other things in the world, came to a complete stop.

Navigating sadness, desperation and uncertainty reminded me
of how poetry is necessary. Poetry and being in community with
other poets has always given me the space to breathe, consider
and to simply exist. In 2021, I decided that Khala Series
needed to continue if even virtually, so the 100 Poem Project
was born. The Centre for the Less Good Idea was happy to
support this project as it revels in work that helps to celebrate
artists in all stages of their lives and practices. Through social
media I issued a call to black women and nonbinary persons
to submit poems dear to them. A flood of applications came
from all over and I was both overwhelmed and overjoyed.
I had worried that I would not receive any applications and
by some great fate 500 people applied. 25 Poets were chosen
to be in this anthology and from their bios you will learn
how these unique previously unpublished poets come from
different countries, have different professions and religions,
backgrounds, and styles; They were all chosen for their magic.

There was no prompt for the applicants and no themes. Poems
came as they were and somehow managed to fit together neatly.

The poems have been housed in five chapters. The first chapter 'Ritual' is a celebration of everyday practices and what we do to get by and get through. Facing a pandemic, practices that bring us back to the center are important now more than ever. From a poem about plantain to a poem about prayer, poems in this chapter manage to find the majesty in the mundane.

The next chapter 'Inheritance' deals with navigating things of the blood. There are habits and features we may inherit and there are traditions we follow and those we break. Dealing with history, memory and heritage seems an essential part of all journeys to the self. Somehow looking backwards every so often helps us look forward more confidently and with better understanding.

The Chichewa word 'khala' means 'to be' or 'to sit' or 'to exist'. In this book's third chapter, 'Being', live the poems that celebrate existence. Here are the poems around body, skin and names and life on the margins. The poets in this series grapple with what it means to exist as themselves, sometimes in love with all that is them and sometimes not.

The last two chapters tackle deep hurt and deep love. Poems around loss, danger and the pain experienced at the hand of governments exist in the chapter 'Wound'. The failing of systems to protect those who live in the margins is central to this chapter. The collection's last chapter 'Tender' gathers poems poems that speak to joy and love as a final note to the reader that these two things are possible. 'Tender' is filled with love poems. Love poems for ourselves. Love poems for others. Love poems for nature. The tender act is opening your heart to joy.

This book is filled with poems for the journey and all your new favourite poets. Through Zoom calls and Google Doc forms and all the conveniences of the internet this book came to be. This book, like the lives of those who have contributed to it, has been woven together with brown thread.

May we all remember the kind thread that ties us to each other. May the poems do their work.

Yours,
Upile Chisala.

Ritual

Other Songs About Home
— *Lineo 'Mile*

I am teaching healing to myself
as a new language
by unlearning the alphabet of my pain.
My mother
sits us at the table to tell us
that forgiveness is essential.
But does not teach us what it looks like
or how to bring it to life
nor how to recognize it in others.

So,
I never learned where the creases fold its face
where the lines trace its palms
but I learn closure as the act
of burying alive a breathing thing.

I am learning not to measure home by place
but rather, the creak of the wooden table
where I sit to make the poems
as much as the poems make me.

This is where the voices aren't shrapnel
making weapons of my wounds
and the stillness isn't holding a blade to my throat.

Here,
silence is the love language of gods
where the heart of my heart obtains its fullness
without leaving others empty,
Where the heart of my heart obtains its fullness.

Pray
— *Rachel Chimone*

And
I'll hold my own
hand
If I need to.

This is how we learnt to pray.

Plantain
— *Susannah S. Alleyne*

The crackle and pop of coconut oil in the pan
awaiting your arrival.
Peeled,
I slice you repeatedly.
Thick enough to fit between my fingers,
Thin enough to slip between my lips.
Laying each yellow piece of you into the hot bubbling sea,
I relish in the sizzle.
Slowly your edges caramelize,
Your middle becomes striped with bands of golden brown
and charcoal.
Silver prongs sink into you,
Turning you over to the sound of more sizzle,
Your other side browning in the heat.
Transformed,
You travel to a desert bed of paper,
Soaking up your oily coat.
Seconds later,
You are on my tongue,
The heat, almost unbearable.
The heat, delicious.
My teeth find their way past your crispy exterior
And to your succulent sugary middle.
Sweetness come alive, *frito*.

I scrub your skin with warm soapy water.
Patting you dry,
My knife divides you in half.
Salt crystals becoming one with the hot sea of fire.
Each half of you slips into the rolling waves,

Small splashes of water begging to be free.
The rising steam fogging up my glasses,
Your honeyed aroma fills my nostrils.
I salivate,
Impatiently waiting for you to beckon me.
Time ticks on and I know,
Until you are ready you are not mine.
I drive my blade into your heart,
You resist but only lightly.
Lifting you out of the oil bath
Delicately,
I strip you of your thick skin,
Your sunset yellow insides greet me.
Your fragrant starchy centre reveals itself.
I slice a small disc of your banana-shaped body,
Steam floats up towards my mouth.
The taste of your fruit holds my tongue in a warm embrace.
I chew softly.
Drifting away,
Surrendering to your sweetness.
Delectability embodied, *hervido.*

— Jennifer Montas

I paid her to braid my hair, but not all strands are made for
fine teeth. She pulled out her thin combs like a magician, rattails
spilling out of her purse - but untangling my hair was nothing
close to a magic trick.

I waited for the white rabbit to get pulled out from under me, to
laugh in my face, to spit out $100 and tell me that this is just the
way it is. To be natural is to be unapologetically you, but I was
being cut at the roots, ending before I even started.

Each tooth grabs at my strands until -
      my fight of a fro - my revolt of a coil -
      my "wrong" type of curl - my rewritten name of a
      nappy headed bit-

until my Hair surrenders,
threads of Her fall into a top hat.

I hold back tears and daydream about breaking her hands.
She finishes. I pay her. I don't bother to watch her leave as I feel
the agonizing scream of my scalp.

    - Texture

Altars
— *Belinda Farley*

not all of us build altars
but some of us do.

some of us
carve calabazas
rub their insides
with honey and cane syrup
then send the offering upstream.
after 21 days
in earnest expectation
of a winning lottery ticket
or the return of a lover long since lost.

not all of us build altars
but some of us do.

some of us
fill drinking glasses with water,
drop blue beads into their mouths
and place each completed effort
in a dusted corner
to dissuade evil spirits
from collecting there.

some of us
hang mirrors within
the hollow of each entryway
to deflect what comes in
that may mean us harm.

some of us
drown our nightmares
within the collection pool
we have placed beneath
the head of the bed frame.
some of us
wear certain colors only
in particular months of the year.

some of us
kiss each bread crust
before we discard it
for blessing after all.

some of us
do not go out of doors
if the moon is experiencing
a suspect cycle.

some of us
bury figurines in our yards
if we want to sell a house
quick and well.
some of us
have worn a smooth place
in the face of the stone
we carry in our pocket.

some of us
believe the silent witness
is always present
but refuses or is unable to speak.
some of us believe
there is a silent witness.

some of us
study the creases of our palms,
brew tea to determine the pattern
of its leaves,
stomp our dollar bills
should they fall to the floor,
apologize profusely should the broom
pass over a foot while we are sweeping.

some of us
burn incense all the time.

some of us
pour a little out before we drink it.

some of us
save our fingernail clippings,
burn the hair that we shed,
collect our tears in tiny vials.

some of us
rest our faith in the rituals
we practice
and we are sustained.
and not all of us build altars
but some of us do.

Sunday Afternoons
— Lewa Letsogile

I take long naps
Long enough to lull my traipsing thoughts to sleep.
My bones breathe again from a week of holding together this brittle soul
Sprawled on my bed I lay
A burnt offering for the washing away of sins
This is where I come for atonement

There's Covid now
My pillow is a church
The dent my heavy head leaves is where I sit
Every breath is a sermon
My lips are adorned in hymns
And scripture like graffiti is scribbled on my tongue
I fold myself into whispers only God can hear

This is where we meet
Strolling along the promenade of silence and peace
The sun smiles widely
Its sits on its celestial seat like a blushing child holding a birthday cake
It blows the candles and dawn sneaks in
making way for another week
And I play hopscotch towards yet another Sunday afternoon

Fell
— *Meron Alefnew*

The pavement turns dark
At half past six.

The trucks of my cruiser
Need a tightening.

For the stones in the road
I inevitably won't see.

Plus:

The frogs that venture
Bravely into the bike lane.
The shepherd urine, golden,
Filling canyon sized crevices.
And the bullsh*t.

My appliances
Need a tune up.
The news cycle mimics
A faulty preset on the washer;
Disappointment, rinse, repeat.

The laundromat is
A half mile away, and
If the machines only take
Tokens of gratitude
on Mondays...

Today, I may come up short.

My shorts need
Extensions now
To fend off ash from knees...
Mask longstanding desires,

Protect longstanding needs.

Autumn air sweeps
Through the vents,
Soothing sister Summer
To sleep.

Meanwhile, in the basement,
The switch labeled

"Fall", seems
Out of arm's reach.

Under dust and dim light,
Motivation is tucked in storage,
Tea kettles are overworked,
And marred white garments
Are strewn about, doused in bleach.

Some feeling around may be in
order this week.

Listen
— LaVonna Wright

I am learning to be loud and it is a healing thing.

Healing, it is
when my body takes up space
in colors that make you tilt your head
in colors that remind me I am proud of my reflection.

Walking with my head held high,
my coils in conversation with the sun,
I can no longer afford to hold my tongue
my vessel,
my hair,
in silence for your comfort.

Healing, it was
when I learned you'd never like me
even if I were quiet.

In my hushed youth, I learned
I am a daughter from mothers who cried in silence
and laughed louder than their pain.
But listen closely
and you'll hear traditions fall.

I am healing and it will be loud.

These Walls
— Mpumelelo Mngadi

So,
I would rather be here
Shivering at the spine,
Holding up these walls that are my home,
Holding up these walls that want to cave in,
collapse,
fold into themselves.

My great-great grand father's home was just like this.
It housed generations.
It kept strangers,
lovers
and friends
intact.

These walls may be crumbling
and cracking
But through these cracks,
the sun offers a flood of kisses.
Still,
I am happy to be here
Cracks and all
Dancing in the chaos of the sun
dancing,
singing,
and crying all at once.

The night,
it too comes bearing gifts,
Gifts I never asked for.
At 3 AM,
the mending begins
and plastering of walls.
Darkness comes with its healing.

And in here,
within these walls,
this body,
this home,
I can dance with the sun rays
and stars
and heal as I go.

— Jennifer Montas

When I close my eyes, I always imagine myself breaking glass.
Loud, sharp, and dangerous – things I always wanted to be.

I've consumed rage to keep smiles from dripping off calloused
faces.
I've broken myself just to swallow me whole again.
                                                    Still.
They say stay delicate,
Keep yourself tender for the feast,
Make sure you bleed pretty.

What about that screams melanin magic?
If feather and brick fall at the same speed,
What is the point of being soft?

Tell me to love myself, then give me every reason not to.
Give me a voice, then steal my tongue –

        watch me speak anyway
        watch me love anyway
        watch my soft turn cruel
        watch me rage

watch you tremble
at how gentle I become with myself –
                at how beastly I become with you.
- *Do Not Go Gentle*

Poetry, The Pain Painter
— Asante Siphesile Khwela

I needed a place for my pain
So,
I turned to these pages.

Before the writing and the feeling things through,
I was obsessed with
The picturesque,
The perception
Of perfection.

And it left no room
For my pain
So,
I turned to these pages.
And padded it into puns,
Laced it in lines,
Left it on these pages.

Until I
Felt safe.

Until I
Felt right.

Visions
— *Anna Thomas*

In peace,
my dreams come.
Waving a flag as white as the moon,
Laying down warpaint and battle cry,
I surrender to them.

In sleep,
they whisper,
breath on my ear like dust.
I, on the edge of my own visions,
am looking for the meaning.

See what this mind has conjured without me?
Anything I catch—word, image, feeling, phantom—
I hold up to my ears like abandoned seashells and listen for a prophecy.
Is not the future filled with them?
A fatal flaw which desire does not diminish.

The dreams,
they repeat themselves,
over and over,
begging me to hold the message;
to understand.
I reach for it every time
only to be pulled away.
My own quick-sand doubt cautions stillness.

I have eclipsed the ostrich.
My head is the sand and the suction,
and the slow suffocation.
See how sand and salt battle within me.
See that I am both the shore and the ocean.
Shallow before I am deep.
And the message,
the answer, my prophecy,
has me desperate for an end
to the struggle.
There is no respite
for those whose dreams are salt mines.

Some nights I hear it
as close as an exhale,
like an oracle compelled to destruction.
There are times when
I think it is my own voice,
raw and feral,
wailing banshee prayers
amplified in empty rooms
turned echo chambers.
I am too scared to recognize it and the mocking direction it moves to.

But once,
I woke to a blue dawn
and the remnants of the voice of God,
telling me to keep going.

- I write to rally

My Pen for Its Thoughts
— Philile Nkabinde

My pen surrenders to paper
more than I do in conversation.
It tells the heaviness first
and other things later.

My pen glides smoother
when it writes about pain,
Not because it wants to
but because it needs to.
It is filled to the brim with Black ink
that has no space left for untruths.
Sometimes the ink leaks from all the heavy.

My pen wants to understand
what I have kept myself from feeling.
Each stroke is an attempt at honesty,
to unquiet the quiet.
To make known the ignored.
So, in search of myself
and my understanding of my pained pen
I will write from the bellowing parts of my core
out of love and necessity.

My pen has this habit of putting to paper the words
I have been holding,
and telling me what aches,
of writing me and rewriting me.

I am still not certain of who is guiding whom
the words, the pen or me,
but what I know is the writing wants to be done
the words want to be found
and my pen
and I
both want to get some of the pain out.

Yours painlessly,
My Pen.

Out of Office
— *Meron Alefnew*

No shadow can exist
Without light
And dishes
Don't clean themselves.
- An African proverb-

Sponge on ceramic
Does much for the mental
Demonstrating how to
Welcome and release
Debris.

And clandestine is she
Who heals at the faucet
And kneels in showers
Inundated with grief, see…

Her name cc'ed
On messages that seem
Void of awareness
Or care.

And to respond today
Requires fingers and neurons
Troops, many of whom
Cannot be spared.

The rebel forces advance.

Safehouse
—*Yemeece*

in this house
we cry
and we aren't afraid to
because we know enough about darkness
and how it can only be followed by light

in this house
we laugh
because we know
joy is not made to be a crumb
and postponing all happiness
is a tough way to exist

in this house
we dance
because the long journeys
our feet have walked
deserves the applause of our thighs

in this house
we re-create our lives
as many times as we need to
because our bodies have carried
enough tragedies to drown us
and here we are still breathing

Inheritance

Our Mothers' Dressers
— LaVonna Wright

My mother's reflection smiles at her in the looking-glass
Inheriting the ritual of dressing herself with perfumes and lotion
And her ancestors' smiles. Her auntie stares back at her, lovingly as always

Lovingly as always, does she regal our matching school photos.
We co-exist with family we do not know
This dresser belonged to my grandmother, before that I do not know

I do not know how the dresser becomes a time capsule
For what we love and have loved. A place of worship
For that love. My mom would tell you she only believes in God

In God's shadow do I find shelter
In God's shadow do we turn to instinct
To honor life lived on top of our mothers' dressers

Our Mothers' dressers
These living altars.

(untitled)
— *Brianna Camacho*

Where does your mind go when it wanders?

Lately...
To inevitable confrontations with past versions of myself,
To questions of motherhood,
And roads not traveled
And almosts.

There is no learning without remembering.

I was almost a mother once,
Sometimes I mourn the lives we both lost.

Keeping secrets runs in families
But I...
I am the disruptor of tradition.

At Least 80,000 Years
— *Belinda Farley*

I've lost my Eddie Mabo stuff : The memo on which was written...
Each detail of that Aboriginal myth of The Three Daughters
Whose father cast them each in stone – in order to save their lives.
To keep them from being eaten, whole.

All I remember is: They are still standing in wait
for the spell to be broken. The details are gone now.
But I believe they became Blue Mountains,
or I believe they'll become Blue Mountains.
But then, I don't remember much.

So on to Eddie Mabo,
and what this is really about:
What this is really about is Eddie Mabo.
And Aboriginal Persons and Indigenous People
and the Baobab tree and mango trees and scar trees
and the trees of Djab Wurrung.

This is about Malo the Octopus God,
who stretched his tentacles across the ocean
and left behind fingerprints of land,
for brown father to brown son
to exchange in salty kisses before the music of a gourd.
While the inner pink flesh of Australia
was throned Queensland,
its skin taut as a boil beneath the Crown.
Until Eddie Mabo.

Until Eddie Mabo, with peppered beard fantastic
in its impertinence sought a personal parcel of Murray Island.
Stood poised to bury his feet in the soil,
sprout roots and become his own tree.
For this he led a Movement.
Refuted rule of law
reading Indigenous People of Australia knew no
concept of land ownership before white men arrived.
Claimed terra nullius to condone colonization.

Is it any wonder Aboriginal People demand their doctrine be spoken?
Their maps drawn in blood?
Knowing death may come before a gavel split
the bench of a country that displaced brown babies
in white orphanages.
Projected screens of propaganda
flashing the shadow dance of their hair, haloed.

Who are the heroes before the graves are dug?
Graves adorned with hibiscus flowers, carved in stone.
Graves befouled in one night's passing with swastikas.
Graves whose marble eyes are gouged out.
This is what happened to Eddie Mabo's grave.

But look, look what Malo, Malo does!
Extends forth once again a lone appendage:
Offers an earthen cocoon to entomb
the man who wanted to root among the sorrel trees,
the mango trees, the trees of Baobabs.
A spirit now walking with roots that sprout from each toenail
like a dreadlock.
Roots slung over one shoulder.
A vigilant soul: Eddie Mabo.

Walking, walking, walking the Land.
Walking, walking, walking the Land.
Walking, walking, walking the Land.

ancestors reprise
— *Ewurakua Dawson-Amoah*

the small of my back
is comprised of all the moments
my ancestors said no.

the creases in my lips hold their
lifetimes,
romances,
lullabies,
pain.

my eyes hold proof of their existence.
my dreams keep their memories alive.

Faces
— Tumelo Thamaga

I wear dead men's faces.
My laugh is my grandfather's.
I look like the other grandfather and his father before him,
Now I am them.

All the great-greats and their sons seem to take turns strutting in my limbs,
Colouring the timbre of my voice,
Choosing my clothes and my tastes.

It is strange for my family to witness their very dead fathers
very alive in my me.
I see it in my father's eyes, I am his father returned.
My grandmother's soft chuckle confirms, I am someone she's known before.
My mother stares and sighs at all the men resurrected through my body.

But to me,
We are as good as one,
These men and I.
And when they were here in flesh, I was them.
Dead men wear my face too.

1919 to 1991
— *Chloé Dinae*

Because my skin is darker,
I was told to marry lighter by my GG.
So my babies wouldn't be too black.
So my babies wouldn't be harmed.
So lighter people wouldn't be afraid.

The truth is my GG,
whose skin was light,
married light and but loved someone dark.

The truth is my babies
would be made in the image of a king
and that would make someone feel very uncomfortable.
Dark black and loved, a scary beautiful thought.

The truth is,
my GG was tired of shaking them up
and receiving no response.
My GG was sick, abused and tired.
Tired of wading in the water and never getting dry.

Now,
my GG has tried to pass on her tried to me
and I just won't take it.
I am going to be dark black and fighting
till my very last day.
And who I love is going to be dark black and fighting
until theirs too.

For Father
— *Anna Thomas*

This tea/chamomile comfort brewed/out of love and then some/
for me/by me/made a memory of
the morning/a flurry of forgotten absolutes/ then left behind/
out of love/for you

This tea/peppermint peaceful brewed/in this kitchen/in this pot/
cotched up between prescription filled countertops/bubbling like
blood/steeping like sleep/left in urgency/of love/ for you

This tea/English breakfast elegance brewed/stewed and
steaming/ in the gleaming light of morning/left imprints on the
words I speak/morning dew on whispers/angels' breath from the
cup/left in search of answered prayers/out of love/for you

This tea/oolong oasis brewed/respite in a cup/made resolutely/
poured decidedly in a mug/my name branded on its side/a finite
detail/a staunchly taken position/budged out of love/for you
You/who command my every minute/sit by/watching the cup
grow cold/watching me pour warmth/watching/watching/
watching me pour comfort down the drain/this tea/my tea/
eclipsed by my love/for you

This tea/black boiling bitter brewed/in dead of night/poured at a
witching hour/no sugar/just spite/I wait till morning/ let it grow
cold as ice/you awake with mouth open/and I watch you speak/
cup finally at my lips/ I drain the cup/out of love/for me

naming ceremony
— *Ewurakua Dawson-Amoah*

i am so proud of my name
the intricacy of it all,
the dramatics,
the way she makes a production of herself.
makes you say her twice
maybe three, four times
just to get her right.
the way
she causes tongues to stumble
and fall,
twist in confusion.
my girl's a labyrinth of lovely sounds,
a symphony
of letters so unfamiliar
to your tongue.

you place my name in a box named "difficult"
and file her into a cabinet labeled "too long".
you store her in your memories as the name that must be
shortened
and prepare your lips to ask
"call i call you by a nick-"
no,
no, you cannot
no, you will not
you will unlock that box
open that file
and study her
until your tongue untangles
and you find your pathway towards her pronunciation.

you will
hold her in your consciousness
until her letters make sense to you
and she slides out your mouth
the way she deserves,
the way
my parents planned for
when they named me.

you see,
my name holds meaning.
she carries a history,
she carries
centuries
of a culture
that i call mine
and when you
shorten her,
fumble her,
bury her,
file her away,
you are burying me.
you are burying
my culture,
my essence,
my birthright,
my name,
and that?
that just isn't gonna fly.

so, hello
nice to meet you
my name is ________
and no, you cannot.

In His Name
— *LaVonna Wright*

My father and I share the same initials
Though I am also known as Child of God.
I wonder when he stopped believing
In me.
I wonder if he knows he is loved.
You say your God is a mighty God.
Mine is invisible.
Silent.
Too much thought makes one doubt.
So, I've stopped wondering
Why he stopped coming to the rescue of His children.
I search for where my identity rests.

God.
My Father.

I cannot see your face.

Poison

— Ashley Rose Scantlebury

I come from a family of addicts.
Born out of men who use toxins as a way to be present.
Raised by men who don't know when to stop
So their bodies just stop for them.

These men who have passions and dreams
But succumb to the pain of their nightmares.
Men who see women as priests and wine as a sacrament,
compelled, they just take both.
They are men who find solace in beer bottles
and make ashtrays from the bottle caps
Innovative,
and inadvertently existing.

To me, their trespasses are dwarfed
by the opaqueness of their promise
and yet they struggle to gaze too long in the mirror.
Their eyes dart around avoiding the
reflections of a pain they did not let go of.
Seeking highs, they lurk down below,
where they can hide from plain view to lick their wounds.
Unanswered invitations pile into small mountains they do not
want to climb,
not every day judged by everyday critics.

Sitting out,
they inhale the fumes of the city's smoke.
They laugh,
Remembering the names of old ghosts
And for moments they lose themselves and all they lug around.

For moments they are free.

(untitled)
— *Lineo 'Mile*

In this story
My [ ] is half man and half wound before I am born, so I spend
my childhood learning to tame my voice, so it does not cause
him to bleed. My mother is married at 22 and given a new
name decided by the names of her children, and my birth adds
a second name to her and another layer to cover up all the
selves she will have to shed to become my mother

★★★

I do not discuss this unless I am asked, but I grew up – Not in
a broken home, but in one that was always breaking. Here we
were nurtured by silence and taught to exist as questions. And
how could we convince ourselves that we were worthy of love,
when we were fathered by absence and mothered by grief? Our
households were warzones, so we were born a burial and have
been existing in the world as obituaries ever since

★★★

But I am home now, and on my third day back my sister and I
watch a film where people toss coins into a fountain for love,
and I know better than to believe that it could ever be that easy;
that it could ever be without the bruising. But my parents are
lonely before I am born and before it can ever be my fault and I
do not get to meet the people who are my parents before it is all
they can call themselves

★★★

I do not meet the man in the photographs whose eyes shut when
he smiles, nor the girl with the split between her two front teeth
who grows her hair in knots. I do not meet her before she is my
mother, with her straight hair, and her three names, and her lost
selves, and I think that I too might be a wound. What else do
you become when you are taught to speak by men who can only
teach a language with their voice in the tone of a blade?

★★★

I do not meet them. But I am haunted, always by the heavy
ghosts of their absence. I am always looking for men to use as
a balm for my loneliness and fill up all the spaces in me that
are shaped by my [ ]. I look for other girls who understand what
it means to be born into silence, and see home as an exercise
in all the ways a person can break like a country at the hands
of another

★★★

But I am made whole again. Because in all the years that my
[ ] spends leaving without ever going, my mother grows her hair
back in knots in protest; and reminds me that we are worthy of
a love that leaves us heavy with healing. That does not wound.
That does not ask whom we have been, where we have been and
if there are parts of us there that are still praying for resurrection

ancestors
— *Ewurakua Dawson-Amoah*

i did not need to meet you
to know
that you make up
the bones in my back,
the power of my tongue,
the music of my soul,
the silk of my skin.

Being

this body
— Zizipho Bam

this body
is a place of love
a palace
built by my entire lineage
an inheritance
great great grandmother chiseled me her face
grandmother mastered me these curious eyes
my mother colored this mind
my sister lent me her heart
a queen's fortress with long limbs
and big black curly hair standing like a crown

this body
is love
a song wrapped in the sweet soft glory of God herself
a testimony
sends me notes about how happy my toes are
shivers in my knees and smiles when it is nervous
feels strong
falls fast
this body

Put Your Big Girl Panties On
— Chloé Dinae

We handle with care,
the ones that get us up.
The ones that cut creases
and take us out of comfort zones.
The ones that are naughty by name.
Slivers of silk and mesh, and not much else.

The ones that have us out at 3AM
to meet our lover after the party.
The ones we grow out of by the 4th hour,
wet from love juices.
We take them off carefully
and slip them in our purses.

And then there are the ones that protect us.
The ones that hug us and
hold our bodies,
fupa and all.
The ones we bleed into.
The ones that know our secrets.
The ones that carry our pee
when our bodies give in to
belly laughter with friends.

The ones we pull down to touch ourselves in.
They roll and rest on our thighs.
Not judging, just holding on till we are ready.
The ones we'll always have to put back on
after lovers and hands, blood, body and laughter.

We live and love in both kinds.
They know us, our dirt and our dirty little secrets.
We put them on.
We are big girls in both.

Taste
— *Rachel Chimone*

We have pacing panthers,
raised as house cats,
caged behind our ribs,
steel where our bones should be.

We wear cufflinks now.
We grew up.

We taste different.
Even to ourselves.

wild woman
— *Teni Adebayo*

wild cobwebbed veins spread across pale strata of skin
how many journeyed on your river nile?
leaving scars and commas—
turning your blood sea blue:
calm. deadly. inspiring
wild woman,
how do you triumph
over hell
and still stand strong
in soul and skin?

name
— *Ewurakua Dawson-Amoah*

to the reader with the long name,

make
them
say it
twice.

Queen
— Belinda Farley

In elementary school
the girl who was picked-on
was named *Reina*
by the Spanish teacher
because she had a name
that did not translate

Imagine
The Black girl with pigtails
hair that stretched
from her roots like a claw
who played alone but laughed
at the jokes she inspired
Named *Reina* this girl
by the Spanish teacher

To the students learning beside her
knee-tucked beneath school desks
Reina! Reina! all day long
Because her name could not be
translated into any other language

And so *Reina! Reina!*
each day in class

And she answered
And we were taught

(untitled)
— *Morgan Tolson*

My skin
is earth
A gift from my ancestors
Reminding me how to
Survive, adapt
Be *rooted* and *grow*
Even in a sea of
alabaster
I am blossoming still

Hungry
— *Rachel Chimone*

I belong to myself first,
and you?
You will not pry me open.

Let your eyes make all the threats they'd like to.
You will not undo me.

You with all your hopes and maybes.
I have my own
starved and
grown.

where do you put your transness?
— *Mpumelelo Mngadi*

Now that you've taken it out the closet,
Where do you put your transness?

When you go home,
Where do you put your transness?
Do you place it just beneath your skin?
Or does it hang a little too much over your shoulder blades?
The last time you let it loose
they called it an identity crisis.

When you walk into the world,
Where do you put your transness?
Do you keep it in your bones?
Do you keep it in your joints,
Your spine,
Every single vertebra,
So, it can hold you up?
Because you know you need it
To stand in a world that wants you erased.

When in conversation,
Where do you put your transness?
Does your transness linger at the back of your throat to correct them?
Does it cover the lining of your belly so you can stomach the violence
you are force-fed
Or do you let your belly swell up in anger?

In the night club,
Do you keep it just below the waist so it can gyrate till the sun come out?

In your loving,
In your living,
In your friendships,
In your day to day being,
In your not-belonging and in your belonging,
In your surviving,
In your joy and in your unrelenting spirit,
Where do you put your transness?

I have some questions
— *Muthoni Mwangi*

God of Abraham, Isaac and Jacob
God of my ancestors... "Ngai"
God of Gikuyu and Mumbi
God of the Israelites who circled the desert for 40 years
God of the Trans-Atlantic Slave trade
God of Emmet Till, Breonna Taylor, George Floyd, Eric Garner

God of the queers
Are you out there?

I have some questions

18

— Asante Siphesile Khwela

i
am in my own arms
holding me,
up together.
and when
my trembling hand thinks
of slipping
my mind tells
my heart
to prepare itself.
it says i
       know
           the
               direction
so   in
when   which
thoughts   things
of   will
angst   go.
try to
gnaw.
greedily
at
my   go.
strength   can
                      things
                 which
              in
           direction
        the
     know
i say i

Heels
— *Chloé Dinae*

As young girls,
we can hardly wait for the moment we'll wear heels.
Idolizing our mother's strut,
We dream of our own walks in them.
Will they make us look as pretty?
As tall? As strong? As woman?

In this dream,
we don't stop to oil our feet
or think of all the pain
and heavy that might come with the shoes.
Woman shoes.

In this dream,
we and our calves are made ready,
There is no hardening.
No wait period between purchase and prance.
No wearing in of shoes,
no pinching at the toe
and no corns formed against us.

In this dream,
the dancefloor knows us the longest
no matter the pair we have on.
We never tire,
or slip them off when the night is still young and breathing.

In this dream,
in heels we trust.
New or used,
towering or tiny,
our mother's or our own.
We only think of the women
we'll be in them
not what they'll cost
or where they'll take us.

A Black Woman's Meal Plan
— *Philile Nkabinde*

Black women eat strength for breakfast
in the morning rush,
when there's no time to warm it up.
That one bite is just enough
to nourish what the misogyny has starved us of.

If we are lucky in the day,
we will see the discrimination and objectification for what it is
and how it is packaged as a sugar-coated treat.
And we will say 'No, thank you.'

At lunchtime, a rumbling travels through our bodies-
an appetite for safety
in a world so White and so man.
This dire hunger for protection is present at every meal.

On our dinner plates,
is a large portion of Eurocentricity and what counts as beautiful;
lies and standards we have always been fed.
Things that tell us we are only beautiful after we straighten our afros
and our words.
Bleach our thick skin and our deep histories.

You see, a Black woman's process of daily dining is different.
We eat for mere survival.

If you as a Black woman ever finds yourself hungry
for safety, for beauty, for space
eat strength
even if you have to serve it yourself.

Survival
— *LaVonna Wright*

Red rose,
Sharp thorns
In my Black hands
Closer to brown
Than the Mother Earth most people imagine.
I've never seen a brown flower
Unless it was leaning towards death.

Life is blooming
And pruning,

Living,
And dying
To the belief
That red
Wasn't made for my brown lips.

Muddy Puddles
— *Ashley Rose Scantlebury*

Visions of her rebirth glimmer in the waters she used to wash her son
Even when **muddied,** the droplets run clear as the day
Her ascension was one that was felt long before it was seen.

To see her is to love the curves of her body,
lines within her palms, the dried milk that gathers in small creases by
her nipple.
Think of her even when she asks that you do not.
When the baby rests and the silences swallow her up whole.

View her from the windows of your mind with new eyes
And watch her flirt with time in shades of purple like the trees do for spring.
When blossoms and bottoms fall to the grass
like old myths about what men like to see.

Time moves as she does, effortlessly
towards this day when she feels soothed in her skin
And connected to the grounding power of self.
She is everything to someone.
She is everyone to me.

Anger
— Elodie Parthenay

my anger is not
a fired bullet,
a punch in the gut,
a slap in the face,
china smashed on the wall of
what we can't bear
to call home
anymore.

my anger is the whistle
of a kettle,
a saucer of milk heating,
boiling over.

my anger is a tidal wave
you didn't see coming until
its shadow made you
disappear
leaving you with
only the knowledge
that everything that used to be
will be annihilated
never to be rebuilt.

you called me soft
when what i am is
liquid.

— Jennifer Montas

I watched white boys bury themselves into a Prince Charming,
white hands playing in silky hair and pink lips.
We of all shades melted at blue eyes and freckled cheeks.
I cried black tears to white romance
wondering
would hands run through my kinks?
Were brown lips too stain to admire?

My love
an impossible reality
an impossible dream.

Black boys never live through romance – dark girls never had a chance.

-Give Us Our Movies

Shed
— Tumelo Thamaga

I keep
asking why
didn't I
arrive in
my body?

Was the
reason I
was born
in this
body to
shed?

Was the
reason I
was born
in this
body to
shed?

Maybe in
this body,
I
can hold
all of them.
To rid what
I must,
to
bring the
sons back.

Or did
someone
make that
decision
for me
when I left
the womb?

Hidden Beauties
— Elodie Parthenay

in a garden
of delicate flowers
i was too brown
i was too tall
too strong
too rough to the touch.

i tried to make myself greener
stunted my growth so as not to threaten,
conform
or break the unwritten rule
known by all
trees
known down to their roots,
they don't belong with flowers.

and as i struggled i wondered
how many of these flowers
were trees in disguise too?
and what if we let ourselves
grow
to be what we were born to be?

what if we
reached towards the sky?
our crowns lush
our bodies brown and rich.
how many of us would there be?
how glorious a forest would we make?
and would they let us?

Wound

Things

— Lewa Letsogile

Your purple robe lies on the sofa
Wanting to be worn
To take form on your body
I picture you standing by the stove
Stirring soup overcrowded with vegetables
I hated it
But it's all I crave lately
I do not want lonely soup that disappears in my bowl of rice
Even the small of your delicious carrot cake stays stubbornly in my nostrils
The walls anchor themselves with your laughter
Your shoes don't want to lose the dent of your footing
Your weird handwriting is marred on my memories
Everything comes alive when you are gone
A life lost but spread in the things you touched
All the breaking out in a requiem
A ceremonial chant
I guess things mourn their owner too

Blackburn, South Point Student Accommodation
— *Zizipho Bam*

Strange things have grown out of the ground.
Stranger things have fallen out of the sky.
A garden sprouts from a single seed
Or a figure offers itself into the air.

Is it possible for a flower to grow inward?
Like the place we go to hide within ourselves.
Is there a special kind of love that comforts the emptiness there?
Are there gardens we have grown only for our hearts to grieve in
Where nobody else enters but our fears and folds?

A story of love and courage is filled with sacrifice.
Makes our feet forget when we are facing ourselves upside down, dangling.
Marks our lives meaningful when we stare with our heads
behind our necks at all that we have left.

I believe she felt the ground was too heavy for her.
I think she knew she could fly elsewhere and never return.
I know, all she wanted was to be as light as air.
Perhaps, to find it, she had to give herself to the sky.

No one ever tells you what to do with the atrocities
— *Kim M Reynolds*

No one ever tells you what to do with the atrocities.
But the impulse is often to
gather them all up,
race to write them down,
race faster to comprehend.

Take days
and weeks
and years
memorizing the atrocities.

Make connections
across corporations,
nation-states,
neighborhoods,
individuals,
your family,
your namelessness,
your stories,
the stories you will never hear from your
grandfather but will see in everything he does.

Remind yourself
that the physical matter is
the despise of you
and that language can't
capture unspeakable violence.
The kind of violence
that makes you go quiet,
the kind of cruelty is so unbelievable

that you wonder why there isn't a revolt every half second (.)

Once you have

gathered up all the atrocities you can hold

in your arms,

you say,

to anyone,

"Look at this (!) (?) (.)"

"Can you believe (?) (!) (.) :

- That the apartheid regime had a biochemical wing of the government that aimed to exterminate Black people and those people just said 'sorry' and kept owning all the shops, corporations, tv stations, newspapers, and land (?) (!) (.)

- There are hundreds of indigenous children under what Canada calls "schools" (?) (!) (.)

- That white people in the US made postcards out of lynchings as souvenirs well into the mid 1900s (?) (!) (.)

- That white nation after white nation has worked tirelessly to suppress and control Haiti (?) (!) (.)

- That Israel forcibly sterilized hundreds of Ethiopian immigrants in 2013(?) (!) (.)

- That Breonna Taylor's police report listed her injuries as "none" even though she was shot 8 times and left unattended and clinging to life for at least 15 minutes (?) (!) (.)

- That George Zimmerman sold the gun he killed Trayvon Martin with for over $100,000 (?) (!) (.)

- That 3 million students go to schools with cops but not nurses (?) (!) (.)

- That the DA Government sent orders to demolish people's
  homes during winter, during a pandemic, during an eviction
  moratorium (?) (!) (.)"

Many (my) people will not need to go far to believe (.),
you will not need to go through any
of the above list.

And when you've emptied your arms
of all atrocities you could hold for that day,
no one tells you what to do
with the ironies that are on your doorstep.

Like
how Cyril Ramphaosa was a trade union organizer
and 30 years later oversaw the murder of 34 mine workers.

Or that Cadillac started funding
Black Lives Matter celebrity activists
who tell us to electric slide across museums owned by
racist-turned-liberal-for-pay white people

Or that Barack Obama humanized many of us
and at the very same moment
vowed to kill so many more of us.

Or that people will get burned
by the fires set in defense of billionaire rapists.

Or that Chimamanda turned out to be the bad guy.

Listing all these things
doesn't seem to change the pattern.
But you keep stacking

because it keeps happening.
As you stack
the violence,
the atrocity,
the catastrophe,
the irony,
they take up all the space,
suck all the air out of the room.
They take up
the size of your kitchen,
then the bathroom,
then every home on the block
Then the whole neighborhood.
Maybe the whole size
of South Africa
or DRC
or Brazil or …

Or maybe at that point,
it becomes clear that it is not about
the atrocities
or
the ironies
at all
but about the question
of where we are going to find dignity
in a world
where the arch of history
bends
towards
those with private security and private property

and will the fire of revolution keep you warm?

Heat
—*Yemeece*

I have been putting out fires all my life
and you dare to ask
why I smell like smoke

Silent Black Girls
— *Pandemela Mathoma*

When the white girls speak out
it makes the news,
lights flash and in come the police
ready to make things right.
Petitions, posters, rallies, searches, rewards,
interviews, questions, suspects, signs, hope.

White girl screams, we listen.

When the black girls speak out,
it's silence, soft cries, anger and curses
so we should just learn our places,
learn to be quiet.

Noise and the right to make it is a privilege
that only comes in the color white.
And a voice is something we can never afford.

When black girls scream,
We don't, we can't afford that either.

A Patri-Not's Love Letter
— *Lineo 'Mile*

A conversation reminds me that maybe
We do not know what it means
To love a country -

And how can we
When we barely know what it means to love a person?
When we were born in a time when there was barely any country
left to love?

We only know through stories
That a kingdom used to stand
Where the ash now touches our feet.

If I'm to love this country,
It'll be only as an extension of my mother
As a reflection of something
I am already fluent in the language of loving.

Louise

— Belinda Farley

Only once have I been to the grave of my grandmother,
a woman I never knew. Who had skin the color of pecan meat,
and black hair that curled up at its ends. I should have nothing
to say about her. And yet, this is what I have to say about her:

I have been to the grave of my grandmother only once.

What is there? What is there in an Alabama clearing? What is
there in an Alabama clearing, culminating in a pathless place?
Where the grass is overgrown, where no immaculate headstones
line to soldier the dead, where no flowers lie as tributary bedfellows
amongst Black Spirits who ate yellow watermelon here.
Yes, the watermelon meat is yellow here. It grows that way
in my grandfather's patch. The most impressive revelation
my inner-city Chicago classmates heard that year. That year,
so many years ago. And I know nothing more, though knowing
what I know now. Differently. A whispered word: Grandma.
Whispered into the ear of my younger sister on every occasion.
Sealing strength in the not-forgetting of inheritance.

What was whispered to me in that clearing? Where the air hung heavy
on the weight of its own stillness; thick as the cotton in the fields where
my family once bled resistance from the fingertip. Where my father stood
planted in his own silence. His eyes misting over, the faintest smile
on his lips, the slightest shake of his head. For what she had taught,
when she could. And for what he had learned, when he did. In their time.

How do I remember that place?
How do I remember his face?
How do I remember that afternoon of grace,
when flying insects burst in humid temperatures?
And I remember: One tree.
Ma'Dear, I am remembering you. The grandmother I have never known.
The young bride framed in a black and white photograph that sits atop
my family mantle, staring back at me with bouquet in hand. Ma'Dear,
I am remembering you. The grandmother I never knew, who, in a black
and white photograph stares back at me from the sofa where she sits.
Baby girl on her lap, three young children beside her. My grandfather's face
turned toward her. She is smiling.
On a couch in a clapboard house in 1953 in Deatsville, Alabama,
a young, Black family is smiling, and I know why and so,
I smile, too. Ma'Dear, I am remembering you. The grandmother
I never knew, who, in a black and white photograph stares back at me.
A woman with skin the color of pecan meat, and black hair that curled
up at its ends. With eyes that shown hazel through a fine-featured face.
A beauty in death, at the age of 38.
Five children, surviving. One husband, surviving.
A family, surviving. And my father, standing at the grave of his dead mother,
with an understanding I have not yet acquired.
Amid a pathless place. We are still led. And I remember: One tree.

— Jennifer Montas

I watch my red roses curl into a dead black.
Watch the world anxious for another grave.

Somewhere
a black girl learns what the word red means.
Bleach hugs her body like a sin, like a devil's hold.

Melanin takes her time before she's torn apart.
Redbones gather at her feet and try to teach her a new dance.

You call us pretty dying things as we rot – and you wait for
something to fill your gut with.

Ain't yall tired of burning flesh?
Of stealing wounds and calling them healed?

- *Red Roses*

Like Good Fortune
— *Susannah S. Alleyne*

"Trouble makes you troublesome, but nothing sets you off
like good fortune."
– Penance Adair, The Nevers[1]

It seems that at every twist and turn, there you are – trouble.
Like the satin scarf I wrap around my crown each night
I try to wrap my head around this,
Why are we not gentler with one another?
When did we become so self-righteous?
Why can't you name your demons too?

Here is the trouble,
we have no empathy
for those who don't
walk,
talk,
look
or sound like us.

But the wind is blowing toward change
And justice
And a new day
And us laughing again
And us caring for each other
And us realizing that another chance,
A chance to make right and good
is sweet fortune.

---

[1] 'The Nevers' created by Joss Wheldon for HBO

Inauguration (2021)
— *Kim M Reynolds*

And they just killed the earth.
And blew out the sun.

I mean can you believe it?
that they just killed the earth and
that they just blew out the sun?

To be white
and nothing else.

It's inauguration day in the most of violent countries on earth
and all these people
are shuffling their feet
and exchanging papers
and smiling through their teeth.

And
I bet at least 40 interns were harmed in the process
and that 300 reporters
stayed up all night to think about how
and what 'the squad' would say.

And
since when did we do such big ceremonies to
switch from Coke to Pepsi?
Don't they got the same producer?
Same manufacturer?
Or at least some shared stakeholders
or stockowners?

And
did Flint make their switch back yet?
Did their lever ever go back up?

And
at the very same hour,
all over the country,
there is less shuffling going on
and more of the same.

And
there are the ones who are gonna smoke an extra pack today,
there are the ones sitting in their living rooms with scours on
their face.

And
there are the ones who will
muster up all the vocab words they can:
                    fraud,
                    rigged,
                    illegitimate,
                    unfair,
                    not right,
                    against my rights.

And
there are also the ones taking up arms
ready to just kill the earth
and blow out the sun in the
name of a god
whose genesis is white.
And war wooed god.
And america was held onto
and reinforced desperately.
And war IS peace
and genocide IS patriotism
and imperialism IS on the list of demands
Where "make america...." (you know the rest)
is just a call for an ethnostate.

And
those of us who the gun is aimed at....
Well, let's find a new sun?
One where we don't rely on it to "shine" on "truth".
Or one that isn't summoned
to beg people act right in the light,
in the day,
in broad daylight.

I,
I will find my own corner,
my own sun,
cause this one...
this one never worked right anyways.[2]

____

[2] 'The Great Pax White' by Nikki Giovanni

when madness is the currency of the world
— *Teni Adebayo*

when blood and defiled humanity
is sprinkled like salt over stew
as standard
and death in soul and skin is looked over
as a natural phenomenon

when dark skin is bartered for sorrow
and children's clavicles are crunched
under the weight of calamity

what worth does life hold?
are there corners free of this choking curse?
is it wrong that i yearn to rest from this darkening deja vu?
this ugly normal?

My Offering
— *Mpumelelo Mngadi*

If ever Africa decides to crawl into my womb and induce a rebirth,
I'd open my legs wide,
I have been fucked too hard for this world anyway.
I'd embrace the agony between my thighs with a smile.

If ever Africa wanted to suckle my bare breast,
I'd nurse it till I am all dry.

If ever Africa decides it needs rest
I'd offer it my arms, cradle it and
put it to sleep on my scarred black back.

If Africa ever gets hungry,
I'd feed it.
Let it have the last crumb.
Let it lick the bowl clean.

Lunes for Nelle
— *Susannah S Alleyne*

My eyes are open
He hurt you
I can see that now

My heart breaks for you
I did not know
You were suffering

Too long since I heard
Your soft voice
High pitch melody

I do not believe
That love dies
Though you are long gone

Now the pain is his
All he shares a bed with
And agony his only friend

His jaw pulling tight
Tears held
Fear behind his eyes

Did we hurt you too?
So badly
We were not easy

We required grace
We loved you
That was not enough

My ears are open
They are hurt
Little hearts tattered

Find another way
Let us love
Each other once more

My Rapist Does Not Know He is a Rapist
— Pandemela Mathoma

My rapist is does not stand out.
He is familiar.
He looks like someone you've known and maybe even liked.
He comes in wolf's clothing.
He is not hidden or hiding,
he has no need or want to.
He lives in the daylight.
He is your normal everyday monster.

My rapist is the boy next door
with the big smile
that your momma likes too,
the one who bakes cookies,
keeps good grades
and good friends,
tithes and prays,
has a firm handshake
and he even drives a Benz, y'all!

He's real sweet with his words.
Acts and looks like he could love you.
Says so too,
without flinching.
Without showing his teeth.

My rapist does not know he is a rapist,
just a boy who thinks he gave me what I wanted.
I just didn't know I wanted it, he says.
And all the bruises, all the marks, and everything after
well, I wanted that too, he swears.

So, his love is a little rough, where's the crime in that? He asks.
We were in a relationship so it must be okay, he argues.

My rapist does not know he's a rapist.
If he was,
Someone would have told him sooner
that "slutty" clothes weren't an open invitation
that a woman's body wasn't made for just him to take.

My rapist is creative,
good with his hands.
He draws chalk outlines of my body to determine the size of my casket
and the mourners watch him in silence
and in anticipation
years before the grave.

Our families have eulogies written in advance.
Everyone with a sorry prepared at the tongue.
The government apologizes ahead of our deaths.

My rapist does not know he is a rapist,
I told you, he is the boy next door
with the big smile
that your momma likes too,
the one who bakes cookies,
keeps good grades
and good friends,
tithes and prays,
has a firm handshake
and he even drives a Benz, y'all!

In South Africa,
believing women comes after the burial
or never,
not before.
Not ever before.

The Earth's Heavy Heart
— Lewa Letsogile

There is a lament lifted high
High above our rooftops
Fading past the heavenly shrubs
And not lost in the clouds, crawling up the arm of God
Breath leaking into the ground
The veins of the earth run dry
We plaster prayer on our cities
New skin over an ailing world
This too shall pass
And we know this too
Suffering is prayer

III for Ras
— *Muthoni Mwangi*

Reaching across spacetime
We are still here
Loving
Crying
Laughing

We are still here
Breathing
Speaking
Reaching
"Before there were clenched fists, there were arms reaching..."[3]

I am still here
I am your friend

---

[3] This is a quote from "Before Clenched Fists" by Ras Mengesha.

Sunflower to Vase
— Zizipho Bam

I wonder,
How it feels to be a sunflower,
plucked from its source
and wander with the wind into
the waters of a vase on a counter.

To be both ornament and corpse between the laughter
To be so beautiful you forget I will wither
To be missing from myself yet stand tall as I mimic a part of me
How to unlearn this beautiful tragedy.

I shimmer for only a moment.
An inevitable drought I will suffer.

Yet you love me still in your denial.
This is not where your love will grow.
My death will be slow.
The kind that prepares you for letting go.

Smooth surfaces and clear water will no longer be the cure
Soon it will be time to turn off the tap.
The sun will ignore my pores and I will wilt without shame
All my sores will begin to show.
Soon you must bring me back to the shade

For my ending to not leave with your Threart, bare.
One petal after the other.

(untitled)
— *Brianna Camacho*

You left your voice behind
in the stack of composition notebooks
I keep in the back of my closet.
I say a desperate prayer
in hopes of making some kind of peace
with the impermanence of it all.

I walk the tender tightrope between intrusion and understanding
when I read them,
those notebooks you left,
to resurrect you.

Tender

Day Break
— Ashley Rose Scantlebury

The sun breaks through the branches
And finds me in my darkness
Sitting
Softly shivering
Between coffee steam
And the last of yesterday's ghosts.

It finds me
And melts the frosted reflection of a city in despair.

It finds me with you
And invites us both to try again,
To wrap ourselves in purpose
And stand within the chaos.

Love Shorts
— *Susannah S. Alleyne*

-Hajimari-
Undulations on
A dancefloor of dirt and dreams
Electricity

-Chukan-
Tides of love and pain
Summer and Fall of our love
Fortification

-Owari-
A shared life well lived
Sacred moments at your side
Forever awaits

Blue Skies
— *Meron Alefnew*

Will they find the lake?
Somewhere beyond trees.
Dark ripples
Like black knees
We all wanted to hide.

Will they sleep or wake?
Under stars,
Stress, or duress.

Sealed eyes
Do their best
With escorting the ache

Lower backs
Slope steeper now.
Lash lines -pressed- with
Murmurs in chests but...

Blue skies await

There,
Amongst
Cumulus beings
Where heavenly souls
Cook up sunnier things.

And for self
A serving love
Brews what once seemed

Innate.

So, at opposite ends
Of fate's dusty spruce counter
They stand by
For a blue sky to go.

Of fate's dusty spruce counter

They stand by

For a blue sky to go.

(Light)
— *Rachel Chimone*

You collect light in your eyes,
That must be it.
How else can you look at the world
like it shines,
even on days it doesn't?

Everything Is Breathing
— *Philile Nkabinde*

When it comes to the matters of the heart,
It is not the heart that gets to decide what matters
It's you, in your entirety
It's you in your pain, joy and power.
It's you,
In your breathing.

See, we breathed together so deeply and closely
That I could taste your pure intentions in the air
And you could taste mine.
You offered me a loud kind of love
That gave my name the echo it deserves.

Your love gave my heart a beat to skip to,
A rhythm to tap my feet to and
A reason to let my inner child come out to dance.

I know we have a date with destiny
And getting to know her means
Doing the heart work
And learning how to breathe better;
How to take fuller and deeper breaths.

When you breathe better,
The world is clearer and quieter.
You can hear God when He prays to you.
You can hear the things He also needs from you.

I also know that even when the echoes of my beating heart
Begin to fade,
The love we share in my breathing heart is still alive.

The language of the heart
Is spoken in inhales and exhales.
Through what we allow in and out.
When the day ends,
Learn your heart
And understand that it is still beating with you
And for you
So, breathe like it.

Trap Doors (I Became it so I'd Never Have to Feel it Again)
— *Kim M Reynolds*

The first thing I did was cut my hair.
I cut my hair
And then
I cut it again.
I cut myself from new cloth
and covered up the cuts,
the broken glass left,
vowing to only look at them in passing
and to never go looking for anyone else's.

Then I got new glasses.
Big frames and thick lenses,
tinted when the sun comes out.
Anything to help with the adversity
and the strain to my eyes.
It was an adjustment
to look away so often.

The next thing I did was go away.
Left on an afternoon train.
Got off at the mall
in the next town over.
There,
I bought :
    4 pairs of cargo shorts,
    6 pairs of Nike socks,
    1 beanie,
    2 caps,
    and 3 sports bras.

I spun in circles
looked at myself
from all angels,
flattened most of my curves,
and bought 3 mirrors
at the shop next door
to set up a carousel of my own
in my home.

Then I decide I want to build a home,
a new one.
I take up carpentry
and learn to work with wood.
I get very good at it.
I build toys
and bookshelves.
I build desks
and tables.
What I build the most of is trapdoors-
I build those into everything.

Everything has a place now,
my new mirrors
and new clothes
and new glasses.
And each room in the house
has at least two trap doors.
They are lined with rubber
and lots of padding.
And the trapdoors make me feel very clever.

Because I made layers
and depth that are for my eyes only.
I am my own architect of protection.
I started calling this "insurance".

I now start calling girls over
to my new house.
And I build trapdoors there too,
between us.
I tell them that I am just passing through.
I do not utter the word "baby".
I do not take pictures in bed,
or in public.
I do not define boundaries.
I do make breakfast in the morning,
but I always have a "meeting"
right after we finish.

And after two years
of these rushed breakfasts,
I think about the cuts on my right arm.
I haven't checked on them in a while.
It seems,
the padding
and the rubber
of my trapdoors has kept me safe
on my way out
of all the moments
I wasn't prepared
to stay in.

As a result,
I have left every person
in the dark of an empty room
I invited them into.
Because I have my trapdoors,
and no intention of seeing things through.
I know in protecting myself
and only myself
I have become the very circumstances
that broke,
cut,
and
fractured me.

I became it,
So,
I'd never have to feel it again.

In(Gratitude)
— *Lineo 'Mile*

I learn prayer as the practice
of believing in changing the mind of God.
In doing so,
I neglect gratitude.
Forget to say I am thankful,
even for you.

I forget how love too
can be an act of worship.
How it was loving you
That brought me close to God
in ways that not even prayer could.
But I recognize you as the echo of a past ask,
the substance of an old plea.
You are the answered prayer
that is teaching my heart to pray again.

Frozen Grapes
by Ashley Rose Scantlebury

I feel myself coming back from death
An ethereal resurrection.
Coming back from the stillness
where I was without myself.

I feel myself thawing,
shedding the droplets of past **traumas**
and creating a new shape.

I am starting to feel everything.
The sting of the nettles that grab me
as I step through dark corners in this overgrown **fortress** I once built.

I am starting to love the breath on my skin,
Kisses on my neck and just letting the bliss linger.
Tender souls collide and fall to undiscovered depths within
Calling for pieces of me I did not know were there.

His warmth journeyed through this once empty vessel
Softening the skin then all the way to the core of me.
And to him.
Committed, we follow the sweet trail of nectar that summer leaves behind.

(untitled)
— *Brianna Camacho*

The sharp freedom in knowing that only this moment is real.
Everything else is an illusion
Or a memory,
And even those you hold dearest can change.
But I have a fear of forgetting
And reminiscing is my vice.

The Truth is
— *Muthoni Mwangi*

The truth is
your ex will move on

The truth is
they'll always have a place in your heart
The truth is
you'll grieve and fall apart

There is no timeline
The truth is
you'll find yourself
You'll find love again
You'll learn to trust again
The truth is
you will move on too

Winter Splinter
— Zizipho Bam

If time is the healer of a broken heart,
I could fill this misery inside a barrel,
let it brew and ferment
till I can swallow the memory of all the places it hurts the most.

If not at the end of it all,
I hope I find myself within this unending numbnesssssssssss.

If I could, I'd build a bridge to the part when your silence is not
offensive.
Or to the part when I can stomach regret.

I'd walk a l i t t l e bit slower towards you.
I'd count the steps I took before I fell
Before you fell too.
Into the
spiraling,
spiraling,
spiraling,
world inside a barrel.

But now we wait for the winter woes to wither.
For the pain to turn a distant memory.
A vintage wine I could drink for a lifetime.

(untitled)
— *Morgan Tolson*

I was home
and yet I was homesick.
The candles weren't as warm
As your embrace.
The blankets weren't as comforting
As your voice
Telling me you feel it too.

Succulent for Sale
— Meron Alefnew

I was there
I was a plant
Overdue
For water.

You was there,
Sorta kinda

Shittin' on
My soul.
I was there,
I was a plant
Oxygen,
Lung's fodder.

Yet in *shame*
You suffocated
Still
Feeling alone.

And what a *shame,*
Porque fuimos.
Paralyzed
By the fear

That once again
We wouldn't have
A pot
To behold.

But I was there
I was a plant
Asking gravel
If my roots could
Grow here.

Now present
We've become
Succulents
With stories told.

Here
— *Asante Siphesile Khwela*

Here
you are holding fear in your one hand
and favor in the other,
while you dance
smiling in sorrow's face.

For now,
here in this perfect lie
it is warm
but it won't be forever.

One day,
your feet will want what's freeing,
your body won't want to bend
or shrink
or cower
or dance around the pain.

You will find just where you
can expand,
explore
and reach your arms towards joy.

The Estranged Guest
— Philile Nkabinde

You have repeatedly circled this block
for long enough.
You have sped past
lessons on the way.
It might be time
to park your fears outside.
Walk through the door
and pay yourself a visit
with loving and longer-lasting intentions.

Ring the doorbell softly,
an innermost you has been waiting to let you in,
to embrace you warmly
and show you all the rooms.

Now that the outside
has quieted
and the door is closed behind you,
and you're as here as you can be,
it is time to listen
to what's inside.

Yes, there will be doors in this house,
in this you,
that you won't want to open,
that your trauma may have the keys to too.
But there's also a clarity here,
rooms and rooms of it and
things that have been waiting for your return.
Here, you can call yourself home
body, mind and spirit.
Here is a home that is yours alone
so address yourself with warmth
and make your visit last.

(untitled)
— *Morgan Tolson*

What's for you will not pass you
But will hold you
Like an old lover
Patiently waiting
Moon after moon
For the universe to align.

Hope can be a heartache,
But *not now* doesn't mean *not ever*.

Your best days are ahead of you,
Not behind you.

You Do Not Find a Love Like This
— *Lewa Letsogile*

This love is tender
Like lovers' breaths layered upon each other
Swollen at the chest with desire
Then out, gently
Like wind embracing trees
A wordless song

This love is soft and firm
Like the grip of a newborn
Not yet open to the weight of this world

This love is uttered in words tongues can't bend to
Held in the breadth of hours and height of minutes spent
deeply together

This love is all I want
Here in this place of becoming and possibility

At the Altar
— *Mpumelelo Mngadi*

The gods of spring are pleased with the fruitful riverbank.
They are pleased with you Moses-ing my legs,
Your apostle-ling between my thighs.
Kneeling.
Praying.
Praising.
Lost down there speaking in tongues.
The river Jordan gushing.
Worship these mountains too.
Pray...don't stop praying...don't stop.
Let's say together.
Aaaaaah...Men.

Palms
— *Elodie Parthenay*

missing their hands
the warm print of
their body against yours
molding you
like something they might love someday
smoothing
every imperfection with
a hot palm.

so
as you drift into slumber
you hold
your own hand
and pretend
that's enough.

Maziso we Moya
— Tumelo Thamaga

Doe eyes.
my light beams to greet yours,
an ineffable force.

Ndiriku wongorora chikonzero chaita kuti ndiku tarise nemamwe
maziso angu.
Pamwe ndiwo mazirudo?
Tarisa masizoangu ese.
Awudi?

Doe eyes,
see my love eyes.
You don't want the one who wants you.

Mother Your Lover
— *Kim M Reynolds*

You cannot mother your lovers.
You cannot mother your lovers.
You cannot mother your lovers.
You cannot mother your lovers.
You cannot mother your lovers.
You cannot mother your lovers.
You cannot mother your lovers.

You cannot mother your lovers for your lovers are not your children.

Your lovers are not for you to carry.
Your lovers are not school fees or doctors' visits.
Your lovers are not needing your guidance.

Your lovers are your *equal.*
Your lovers are your friends are your lovers are your companions
even if just in the night,
your lovers are your lovers.

They are someone who dishes up for you
when it's their turn.
They are an equal participant in the planning
of your trips away
in fast cars with arms wrapped nicely around your shoulders.
Their occupancy in your mind must be one without insecurity
and they must see their occupancy as that of spectators,
always looking to see what's going on.
Asking questions in the silence after sex
and taking note of how you respond.

Your lover learns you, as you learn them.
In this way,
they are not your child who takes from you,
who you provide to endlessly,
whom you give allowances
and worry about the conduct of their life.
That is for your lover to do, for they are not your child.

Mothering is love,
but it cannot be the default expression
to your lover
for we know
the burdens and barriers of motherhood.
Of the thankless work,
of the endless work,
of being the driver of the car
and the cleaner of the car
and the GPS
and brakes too.

Being a mother
reinscribes motherhood
and its impossibilities.
The best lovers can transcend
and together
charter the map
of care and love,
but you cannot be a mother to your lover.

You cannot mother your lover
You cannot mother your lover
You cannot mother your lover
You cannot mother your lover
You cannot mother your lovers
You cannot mother your lovers
You cannot mother your lovers

You cannot mother your lovers for your lovers are not your children.

Sticky
— *Chloé Dinae*

She taught me
that when it comes to love,
"You will catch more bees with honey than with vinegar".

But what she didn't teach me
was just how to find bees or
how to know them from rats.

showing up for my soul
— *Teni Adebayo*

I want to be at the
frontlines cheering my soul on
strengthening her when she is sour
and reminding her that there are sweet seasons
still ahead

Music to my Ears
— Tumelo Thamaga

There's a rhythm your heart skips to.
Full and filled,
your chest rises warm.
A beckon to the light.
It hums and sings back.
A soft reflection of each other.
Colouring and complementing,
A silent acknowledgment of a piece of self-music only you can hear.
"Ahh did you hear that?" you ask.
No one else seems to at first.
"Yes, I heard it too" your spirit answers with a smile.

Nameless

— Pandemela Mathoma

It is strange because you will love them
and they will not know your name,
but you will know theirs.
Know it so well that it comes to you in your sleep
and you repeat it like a mantra.
Repeat it
and make a home of it.

You will lose some of yourself in the chanting.
And give some of yourself to a name
that has no business being in your mouth.

You will carry this name, the one that doesn't belong,
between your teeth
gently,
as softly and as sincerely
as flower petals caressing each other in the wind.
You will protect this name against other names.

And still, they will not know yours,
Let alone carry it in prayer or in pleasure or in conversation.
Your body, that they will know
and might even remember after they held it,
stroked it with the skill of a violinist
and pretended to love it in the night's light.

When you have tried everything and
possibly failed to keep them from leaving,
their name will stay with you,
Cling to your tongue
and memory.
Isn't that strange?
Isn't that just in your wonderful nature?
Keeping a name sacred long after a love.

Keeping a name.
Keeping a name sacred.
Keeping
a
name
sacred
long
after
a
love.

Morning Light
— *Teni Adebayo*

morning light gathers on
the grooves of her soil
she weeds out yesterday's pain
hope like beams touches her

and in those redeeming rays

the sadness behind her pupils might not stand a chance.

Snakes and Ladders
— *Asante Siphesile Khwela*

                  The way up isn't always straight
Or simple,
                        Often, it's risky and it winds.
Often it tears you in two.
               'A divided duty'.
                            One you surely owe
                                     To yourself,
                            Another you think
                        You owe to everyone else

Remember,
                    You started this journey alone.

               And for many parts of the story
            Everyone else watched it while you lived it.
This, all you are -
                  This came to be because of your strength
            Your persistence
                       Your perseverance

                   Your prayers
                         Your
                           YOU

(untitled)
— *Anna Thomas*

Life has felt like a desert that always promised water.
I told the sand, "I am not delusional."
And each grain whispered
"There are parts of you that will never be satisfied."

There are times I feel the hand of desire grip the back of my neck,
but call it hope and press on.
I have been sinking here in this nameless place,
born into a clenched fist of want
from which sand is endlessly pouring.

Watching my fingers stretch towards straws,
and sand,
and stars,
going on about horizons and miracles
and water—the ever-present drive to escape my troubles,
quiet the demons,
and quench my thirst—mirages.

I am tired of my own promises.
One foot in front of the other, yes,
but each step shatters yesterday's hope.

"Today will yield a dawn I can be happy in."

With every new promise,
sand becomes the ash of dreams.
Ashes and splinters
and dust—not even words last in the wilderness.

I am tired of the things I hold to.
And yet, how can I stop believing in the horizon
when it is the only constant thing in this wasteland?
The only fertile thing I know that I will wake to.
For all my unbelief,
the steadiness of life,
of faith,
is that which is constant.

How illusive the horizon feels
and how immovable.
Does it make me weak to trust that I will one day reach it?
Does thirst make me a coward?
Bless the cowardice then.
I have been too afraid to give up
the thirst, the want, the promise.
I have left pieces of me in the sand
at the mere thought of water.
lost causes here, perhaps.

But there are more footprints behind me than ahead of me.
So, I hold to my cowardly hope
for the moment when the desert runs out of sand
and tell myself that I will find them,
those lost pieces, again.

They are waiting for me past the sun.

Sister
—Yemeece

we call each other 'sister'
because i get you and you get me
and in our confessions and secrets
we are safe

between us
pain is liquid
allowed to flow
we can sink into our fears
and call our anxieties bluff
we can celebrate our survivals
hard as they were

sister
we can talk without talking
and watch our shame melt
because our spirits sit with each other
in communion
and God joins in trinity

i call you my sister
because these are not just words
unfolding from my hands
this is a revelation
where you and I
are the language
and the dream

— Morgan Tolson

You weren't who I expected
But always what I needed.
Pouring love back into me
That I had siphoned out.
Reminding me that this time isn't like last time
That it's possible to grow together
Without growing apart.

—Kindred spirits

Solar

— Pandemela Mathoma

Our love is encircled by a body of wasteless space,
a gathering of galaxies surrounds us
and as these celestial bodies glide past
I know that love is infinite and everlasting.

As creatures of mother earth,
all we can do in our tenderness
is to teach them how to love.
We will teach them how to love until
there are hearts engraved into their skulls
right where you and I left the lesson.

We will show them that the stars know how too,
as they find each other and align themselves
and the atmosphere does what the atmosphere does
to lungs and moving bodies,
things touch and shine and explode and are reborn,
this, I think tells us just how to inhale and exhale love.

If only lifting up your eyes up to the sky was enough
to see how things are much larger and more complicated
than we make them out to be.
We'd show them the night, and map out our lives
through constellations
tell them just where we were connected and why and how
like the sun, parts of stars long gone
exist in us too.

In a Land Called Hope
— Anna Thomas

In a world
yet to be discovered
is a place
set deep in a valley
a cleft in the rock, a refuge, lighthouse, lantern, a brandishing of stars
a warmth in the night; *we know that where we are going is real.*

We need no precedence, no proof.
We, born out of faith
and into faith,
from faith
and with faith
know it without having to see it,
for within the marrow of our bones is belief.

In a land called hope,
a place that is a promise kept.
A place of milk and honey,
of soap and silk.
We, with bodies filled and laughter loud,
our chests with sunshine pouring out, - see, joy at the zenith.
Where our sorrow finally meets our delight.

Here, in this place
we will sit together and hold hands
sipping on sweet drinks as the sun sets
silhouetted against an endless horizon.

Far away, in a land called hope —
where a body does not have to endure anything more than itself—
there will be rest enough for all the coming generations.

Confession
— *Muthoni Mwangi*

I am a hoarder

I keep pretty tops I barely wear
I keep the jeans I wore the day when that wonderful thing
happened to me
I keep a button with your face on it
I keep messages
I take pictures

I want to save the moments

I keep notes from my desk mates
I keep my diaries from my teenage hood
I keep memories
I keep pain
I keep your words
The twitch in your brow
I keep your smile
I keep your laugh
How your eyes twinkle in a certain light

I keep the texture of your hair
and the memory of my fingers running through it

I keep the arch of your back
The whisper in my ear
The weight of your body
I keep the sound of your breath
I keep the twitching of your legs
I keep your screams
I keep your tears
I keep your pain

I keep your words
I keep your words
I keep your words
I keep the tone, the anxiety
and the loss

I am a losing thing
A lost thing
I keep it all
I am afraid of being alone
Of solitude
(I am my mother)

I keep these parts of my lovers hoping they'll make me whole

(untitled)
— *Brianna Camacho*

Love can exist without lasting.
He taught me this in incremental exits,

Then named his daughter in my honor.

Haworthia
— *Elodie Parthenay*

ever since you left town
i've been growing things
i've been growing myself
big fat roots digging into a fortified soil
ripe fruits bent towards the sun
the pleasures of a simple life well-lived
every living thing thriving except
that plant you gave me on your last day
this one's a little bitch
hell-bent on not surviving
refusing to comply
i scream at it as i sweat to
please it
i've changed its soil its pot its water intake
gave it too much attention
then too little
folding myself to fit needs i can't comprehend
it's personal at this point
maybe it's a lesson in adaptability and patience
maybe i just don't know when to call it quits
maybe i should learn to let a good thing die
maybe i'm the one who's silently unsatisfied
wishing my handler would mind-read my needs and desires
dying a little each day it doesn't happen

Metamorphosis
—Yemeece

Everything beautiful comes from the dirt.
The butterfly.
The gold.
The lotus.
The earth.
You.

Poet Bios

Anna Thomas | **@thepoetscorner46**

Anna is, and always has been, in love with words. Her love of poetry hit her like a train in high school and she has never been the same since. She loves to write poetry as well as experience the words of other poets. In 2017, she started a poetry review channel on YouTube to share her passion with the world. When she's not writing poetry, you can find her in bed watching a K-drama or reading yet another book.

Asante Siphesile Khwela | **@asantekhwela**

Asante Siphesihle Khwela is an artist, a poet and an honest aspiring South African writer. She scribes her growing pains into pages and laces them into lines. She is the kind that never goes a day without tea and spends her Saturdays thrifting and in libraries. Her works are an embodiment of what it means to live boldly and daringly through growth, through youth. Writing is a window in her becoming who she is called to be.

Ashley Rose Scantlebury | **@thechaosofitall**

Ashley Scantlebury is a poet, mother and natural social activist. Her sometimes "gritty" depictions of everyday life have seen her write and publish two anthologies and perform poetry to public audiences, most recently on BBC Radio 5. Her greatest joy is to give words to unspoken conversations and a platform for the unheard, no matter how dark the topic of discussion. She is a creative soul who revels in the feeling of freedom, which is how her art makes her feel. She uses poetry and other artistic mediums not only to unpack her detailed thoughts, but also to call others to freely explore a new narrative.

Belinda Farley | **@poeticbelinda**
Born and raised on the south side of Chicago, Belinda
Farley spent her childhood summers on a farm in Deatsville,
Alabama surrounded by a loving and generous family.
She graduated from Drake University. In addition to
being a published author, she has worked as a newspaper
reporter, El train conductor, schoolteacher, and pub
waitress. She currently writes and resides in Harlem.

Brianna Camacho | **@bri.cam**
Brianna Camacho is a Crucian born (St. Croix, USVI)
20-something person of Afro-Caribbean and Puerto
Rican descent. As a daughter of two diasporas, poetry has
served as an outlet for Camacho's radical self-honesty and
preservation of memory. Brianna has a background in
biological sciences and laboratory research. Currently on
a long detour from a pre-planned pre-med life, Brianna
hopes to bridge the gap between science and softness.

Chloé Dinae | **@chloedinae**
Chloé Dinae is a writer and poet currently living in Atlanta.
She first started writing as a kid growing up in Detroit when
her grandmother suggested poetry to express her emotions
after a fight with a friend. Fast forward a few years, and Chloé
started studying at Howard University, where she met her
college sweetheart, got married, and had her son at 19. Soon
after, they moved to Harlem, her husband's hometown, and
she finished her studies at the Fashion Institute of Technology,
graduating with her degree in Advertising and Marketing
Communications. Chloé spent the next ten years living in New
York, where she cultivated a hunger for cultural landscapes and
art, which is often reflected in her writing. Recently, Chloé has

fallen in love with writing again after going through a divorce. Writing has helped her to connect with herself and begin to explore her new life. After ten years of marriage, she wasn't used to being on her own and struggled with the adjustment, especially when her son was with her ex-husband. Writing has been her main escape through the entire process. Chloé writes about what she experiences, sees, watches, and reads, from divorce and family to romance and race relations. While most of her pieces are about the facts and her real experiences, occasionally, she explores the world of fictional writing. When she isn't writing or at her day job in pharmaceutical research, Chloé enjoys reading, doing yoga, and meditating. She loves astrology and is a Pisces sun, Capricorn moon, and Virgo rising.

Elodie Parthenay | **@elodiewrites**
Elodie Parthenay is a Canadian poet and writer. A former magazine Editor-in-Chief, she studied creative writing at UCLA, where she was nominated for the Allegra Johnson Prize for Fiction for her work on an upcoming fantasy novel. A hopeless romantic and die-hard optimist, she writes poetry about love, loss, sisterhood and self-love, as seen and experienced by a queer woman of colour. Her first poetry collection, The Sun Always Knows Where to Find Me, is a story of growth that encourages the reader to cultivate their own particular magic. She currently lives with her daughter and their fluffy rescue cat, Flerken, in Montreal, where she practices mindfulness meditation, leads the Blooming Writing Workshops.

Ewurakua Dawson-Amoah
Ewurakua is an artist who doesn't compromise with art. Her message comes in the form of poetry, screenplays, short films, and sound desgin. She loves bridging traditional art

forms and new media to claim her message: a melopoeia to sing a new story for the girls and women who look like her. Ewurakua recently graduated from New York University's Tisch School of the Arts. During her time in school, she noticed disparities in representation on and off-screen. In 2020 she launched The Melacast Network, a platform focused on connecting BIPOC actors, directors, and crew of color with the opportunities, talent, and resources needed to tell culturally rich & diverse stories in film. Her work has been recognized in numerous film competitions, including Fusion Film Festival, Raindance Festival, Cinequest, Toronto Black Film Festival, NFFTY, and the Tony Hawkins Award for Excellence in Sound Design. In August of 2020, her short film "To the Girl That Looks Like Me" was named a finalist in the Alternative/ Experimental category of the 2020 Student Academy Awards.

Jennifer Montas | @**je.montas**
Jennifer Montas is a young beginning poet currently studying at Eastern Illinois University topursue a career in teaching and creative writing. Jennifer has previously placed Gold for two Scholastic Art and Writing Awards and one publication for her poem, Glasses. Soon, Jennifer is hoping to publish her very first poetry book, Do Not Go Gentle.

Kim M Reynolds | @**kimberland_1**
Kim M Reynolds (she/they) is a Black and queer critical media scholar, writer, and cultural worker from Ohio in the US, based in Cape Town, South Africa whose work focuses on the narrative and critique of Black arts and politics. Kim holds two master's degrees in critical media and Black and African film from the London School of Economics and Political Science (LSE) and University of Cape Town (UCT), with distinction.

She focused on discursive colonialism in popular culture and news, Black and African feminist studies and Black queer theory, Black film, and photography as an a liberatory tool in Black imagination (see Becoming photo series). Kim is currently a freelancer writer and poet, guest lecturer on critical media analysis, and is co-lead of the research and organizing collective Our Data Bodies, which examines how technology and big data reproduce racism and what community solutions emerge from that examination. Kim is also a co-producer of Blackness and Dance, an independent study on Black identity and dance for radio in Cape Town. Lastly, Kim is an artist fellow with the Octopus Program and the Centre for the Less Good Idea producing a body of work that focuses on 'alternative routes', that being identifying colonial scripts in popular culture, and identifying exit routes from discursive colonialism through large scale installation and text-based work. Their written work has appeared in New Frame, VICE, Black Youth Project, Arts24, Teen Vogue, Outwrite (flash fiction) and others.

LaVonna Wright | *@_lwright*

LaVonna Wright is a poet by nature. Based in Georgia, LaVonna is a womanist, writer, and second-year graduate student at Georgia Southern University pursuing her M.A. in English. As a scholar, LaVonna is interested in the intersections of Blackness, identity, and poetic forms. As a poet, she is inspired to tell unspoken truths about identity as it exists within Blackness, womanhood, love, and trauma. She firmly believes in the value of poetry as a vehicle to discover one's voice. She is currently working on her debut poetry book and her master's thesis. You can find out more about LaVonna and her work on her website, lavonnawrites.com.

Lewa Letsogile| **@lee_letsogile**

Lewa Letsogile is a young aspiring Motswana writer who loves short story writing and poetry. Writing has become second skin to her as she uses it to make sense of the world and her emotions. She contributes to sunrise moment blog and manages the page. She is passionate about mentoring young kids and has been a part of team of tutors that focused on underprivileged children. She studied a BA with majors in Economics and Accounting. When she's not writing she likes to bake and take long afternoon naps. She believes the order of serving cereal is pour milk first then cereal. She wishes to publish a bestselling book one day.

Lineo 'Mile | **@lineo.mile**

Lineo 'Mile is a 22-year-old Rwandan - based writer and storyteller from the Kingdom of Lesotho. She describes her writing as a medium through which she makes sense of and navigates the world. As a literature and poetry enthusiast, she gains inspiration from the work of other authors and is always striving to improve her own. She has been featured in publications such as Button Poetry, where one of her poems was selected for the publication's 2020 Short Form Contest. She is also the co-organizer of a Lesotho-based performance arts initiative, Type Your Art, which strives to improve the visibility of artists and storytellers within the country.

Meron Alefnew | **@meripoppinz.pen**

Meron is a music loving, tea drinking writer from Texas. She writes to capture and package her observations, both internal and external. Meron is a first generation Ethiopian-American. She is studying for a master's degree focused on sustainability and social impact. Her work ranges from

commentary on identity and black womanhood in Africa
to the parallels found between humans and earth.

Morgan Tolson | **@belle.levaux**
Morgan Tolson is a biracial womxn writer from Kansas City,
Missouri. She recently graduated from the University of
Edinburgh in 2020 with a degree in English Literature and
Classics. Morgan's work is often inspired by breaking cycles
of intergenerational trauma, the resilience of the human
spirit, and her ever supportive boyfriend Fergus. When not
writing, Morgan is devouring true crime podcasts, looking
up cute dog videos on the insta, and taking transatlantic
flights back to the UK—where she lives for half of the
year. All while consuming copious amounts of coffee.

Mpumelelo Mngadi (They/He) | **@simp_ly_trans**
Born and raised in KwaZulu Natal but currently working
and residing in Cape Town, Mpumelelo Mngadi is a
24-year-old Black, Transgender and Non-Binary graduate
from the University of the Western Cape. A part time
pharmacist and full time creative, their current focus is on
poetry, photography, writing and being a Trans activist.
Writing has provided him the opportunity to express the
truest version of themselves. He would like their writing
to be a voice for marginalized folks from all spheres of
life. Believing in the power of authentic representation, he
hopes that people see themselves between their lines.

Muthoni Mwangi | **@m.uthoni_mwangi_**
Lisa Muthoni Mwangi is a poet, writer, organizer and student
who is interested in working for freedom in all dimensions and

throughout all time. She is currently a student of Philosophy and Development Studies at Strathmore's School of Humanities and Social Sciences. As a poet she has performed as a featured poet on the "Paza Sauti: Poems for the Start of the World Series" and has published poems on her blood. Muthoni, like Field Marshall Muthoni, roots her beliefs and praxis in the search for community-driven and feminist-led radical freedom for her country, her continent and her people.

Pandemela Mathoma (She/They) | **@pandemela.mathoma**
Pandemela Mathoma is a 17-year-old queer, black womxn, poet and proud Pan Africanist. They were born in Johannesburg and spent some years in Mali before moving back to South Africa. Mathoma's writing journey begun in grade 9, learning through a poetry writing exercise assigned by a teacher how cathartic this form of writing can be. Over time, Pandemela has used poetry to help themselves and others to share their stories and address issues close to their hearts. Mathoma enjoys performing their poetry live for audiences big and small.

Philile Nkabinde | **@philile_nkabinde**
Philile Nkabinde is a creative, namely a copywriter and poet, by profession. By nature, she is an expressionist and intersectional feminist whose melanin pops proudly and severely. She seeks to express the inner world of self and deeper pockets of emotion through her writing. Her work takes the form of written poetry or prose as well as spoken word accompanied by variations of sound and visual elements. When she is not writing nor performing poetry, she will be found in her third natural habitat; practicing yoga and meditation while being lovingly embraced by Mother Nature.

Rachel Chimone | **@rachel_shingai**
Rachel Chimone is a second-year Chemistry student who aspires of later studying medicine. Interested in understanding how things work at their most quantifiable root of existence and how this knowledge can be used for the betterment of others lead Rachel down this road. At a young age, Rachel began writing creatively dabbling in poetry and other forms of storytelling to express themselves. Through writing Rachel has discovered how the ugly and the messy is not only part of but essential to what makes us human.

Susannah S. Alleyne | **@solangeandriel**
Susannah is a poetry-loving, storytelling Black woman living in Western Canada. She came into the world on the twin-island Republic of Trinidad and Tobago, a slice of paradise she still affectionately refer to as home and go back to as often as she can. In this life she is fortunate to be a beloved daughter, loyal sister, devoted aunty, wife and lover, true friend, passionate lawyer and advocate and fan of all things food. Her lived experiences inform her poetry – from daydreaming about her favourite dishes to mourning the loss of relationship with loved ones still living.

Teni Adebayo | **@teniadebayo**
Teni was born and raised on the sandy shores of Nigeria-somewhere cuddled within the refreshing out-pour of family and faith. At a young age, she would curl on the staircase writing and drawing short stories. She has always loved words, it was more than an escape from a sometime monotonous life, it was an expression of her mind, body and soul. One she's learning to exist wildly in. Her favorite words are grace and love. Teni yearns to live her life as a window to reveal the endless love and grace of one man, Jesus.

Tumelo Thamaga | **@naledithamaga**

Tumelo is a consummate creative, with a keen sense of perception and a deep understanding of African cultures. Ever the student, she holds an honours degree in Journalism and Media studies with a specialty in Television. Currently she is undertaking training in African Spirituality and hopes to use this knowledge to further the understanding of indigenous tribes on the continent. A filmmaker, poet, youth mentor and co-founder of a multimedia production company, Thamba Creatives, she aims to focus on stories of African identities untold. Over the years she has garnered experience both in front and behind the camera, also having learned the commercial aspects of broadcasting and stage production. Her skill set includes video production, video editing, feature writing, screenwriting and concept art. She envisions creative works that use colour, light, and sound play to share hidden narratives. This is what 'dear friend' does. Her first light documentary 'dear friend' has showcased at various local and international film festivals, most recently at the United Global Youth Pride Festival and Toronto Queer Film Festival.

Yemeece | **@yemeece**

Yemeece is a Nigerian-born writer and poet. Her work focuses on self-awareness, grief, healing, emotional intelligence, mental health, nature, and other shared human experiences. She is the author of Stirred by Life, her first collection of poems. She currently lives in New Jersey.

Zizipho Bam | **@zizipho_bam**

Zizipho Bam is a South African poet, writer, and visual storyteller currently based in Cape Town. Born in 1996, the award-winning writer creates work that seeks to heal self from mental illness, love, loss, and physical trauma. Navigating through the world as a young black womxn, Bam aims to investigate self and reveal how we relate with one another and the world. Using the body and its experience as inspiration, she reimagines pain to rewrite her experiences into a work of art. The life of her work transpires to visual storytelling, in 2020 the short film God Body, was released and screened at the Gauteng Film Commission Online Women's Film Festival and Behind Her Lens Online Film Festival. She has performed on stages across the country, even gracing online audiences in Washington DC. During the national lockdown, she was in the top 3 of the Poetry Africa 2020 Online Slam Competition. Recently, her poetry has been published in collections like the June 2020 New Coin Poetry Journal by Rhodes University which she also worked on the cover art for the anthology. She also appears in the newly released Yesterdays and Imagining Realities: An Anthology of South African Poetry by Impepho Press, a collection of 30 poems from South African poets under the age of 30. Her short play My Bleeding Thing showed at the National Arts Festival, The Virtual Fringe in 2021 and she was 1 of 3 South African poets that collaborated with Amarula on their new brand expression this year. Bam continues to create and experiment with different forms of writing as she balances being a copywriter and poet every day.

Advance Praise

"I have known Sheila since we were 5 year old's in dance class together. She has lived a varied life of elevated achievements and excelled at every point. She is honest, courageous and you can trust her narrative. It models authenticity! We desperately need this sort of dialogue in today's world in order to help others of us better understand the transgender experience. Sheila has the perfect voice for this."

—CANDY MARCUM, LPC-S, LMFT-S, LCDC

"Sheila Grace has lived a remarkable life. As a paratrooper and a kidney doctor, she chose the edgiest situations within a traditional path. She was all set for a comfortable retirement with her wife and two daughters when she discovered that she was really a woman and set forth on an uncharted journey. In A Calling from the Bones she shares her life with generosity and insight. It's a profoundly enriching read that I recommend highly."

—REBECCA CAMPBELL, CEO, AUSTIN FILM SOCIETY

"I have known this person for 45 years. Her industry, integrity, friendship and smile have been constant and exemplary. Sheila Grace will carry these forward, and the world will be better for it."

—WILLIAM MORRIS, MD, PEDIATRIC
NEUROSURGEON AND USMA CLASS OF 1973

"In A Calling from the Bones, *author Sheila Grace gives voice to both the fragility and unrelenting forcefulness of the cycle of life. Within each of us is a calling, whether and when we choose to heed it determines the authenticity of our life journey. Paths taken, not taken, detours and depots...all are explored in this provoking collection of intimate essays."*

—DANA MINNEY, AUTHOR *"THE ONE MINUTE PARENT"*

a calling from
the bones

sheila grace, m.d.

SHEILA RISING BOOKS

COPYRIGHT © 2018 SHEILA GRACE

All rights reserved.

A CALLING FROM THE BONES

ISBN   978-1-5445-0101-7 *Paperback*

978-1-5445-0100-0 *Ebook*

Contents

Biography

Born and raised in Texas, Sheila Grace, MD, was aware of gender incongruence at a young age but had no concept of what the process represented. Like many transgender women, she aggressively pursued alpha-male activities which effectively dampened the episodic urges to be a woman.

In high school, she was captain of the football team and a finalist for a state Young Texan of the Year award. She attended a large university for one year and was elected the class vice-president. She went on to a service academy, where she was captain of one of the major sports teams and ranked high in the Corps chain of command her senior year. After graduation and Infantry commission, she received her Ranger tab and served for four years as a paratrooper. After a distinguished military career, she earned her MD, completed exhaustive training, and became a respected physician and partner in two well-regarded nephrology practices.

Notable accomplishments include co-founding a

branch of the National Kidney Foundation, receiving an appointment to serve on a state council, and being elected as an advisor to the West Point Association of Graduates. After a medical mission to Africa, she and family created a 501c3 which funded construction of a new wing of a rural hospital in eastern Uganda. Upon retirement and a trip to Tibet, she became executive producer of an award-winning documentary, was elected as an officer for the Austin Film Society, and created Sheila Rising, LLC, a film production company. She now volunteers as a physician at Kind Clinic which offers free gender care, is involved in scientific research on transgender health initiatives, speaks to groups about her own transgender journey, and continues to write.

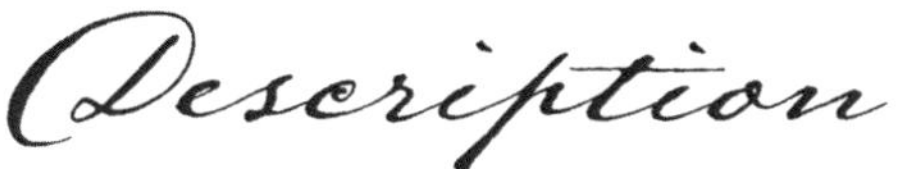

Description

A Calling is an inner urge toward a future life one is not yet living. We each have one, but most of us ignore it. Perhaps we are not listening. Perhaps we are too busy. Perhaps we are afraid.

Yet, there are a courageous few, like Sheila Grace. She felt the resonances of her Calling throughout her life, but pushed them away and sought to live small. But the day came when ignoring them was no longer an option.

As an act of survival, she cast off the uniforms and masks she had hidden behind for decades; her West Point regalia, her army garb, her doctor's lab coat, and the clothes she wore as husband and father. Now she wears the elegant colors of a warrior woman who is honoring her own truth. Such commitment seems to have drawn a host of honest mentors and memorable travelers to her. People, who despite all obstacles, live with the greatest integrity.

Her stories remind us that we feel authenticity first in our bones, then in our hearts. In the spiritual desert we

are seemingly in, it is the one thing that quenches that deep thirst in our untended souls.

Acknowledgements

This book is dedicated to my family. I could not imagine better people to accompany me on this long road home. Our journey together continues to teach me one thing: "love bears all things". I especially want to acknowledge my brother and his wife. They have been among my strongest supporters and shining beacons of hope. They were there to provide constant love and support in the darkest of days. Without their encouragement, this book would not have been written.

I want to recognize the many loving and lovely people that I was honored to know during my years in the practice of medicine. They were my mentors; and, the things they taught me now sustain me in a time of great transition. I cannot be grateful enough for what they have brought to my life.

I am so very grateful for the emotional and spiritual guidance and support that has come from a group of therapists, friends, and co-workers. Chief among those are Dr. Wynette Barton, Dr. Kitty Harris, Dr. Jared Dempsey, Vernon F. Williams, MD, Mary Guerrero-Cox, Sarah Meinzer, Dana

Minney, Shannon Yanacek, Janie Forister, Lee Macmurdo III, FNP, Marcy Keefe, NP, Alan Berg, John Robison, Brad Pittenger, Cathryn Hunter, Rebecca Campbell, Linda Middleton, and Mike Wood.

There is also a special group of professional women who have become some of my best friends through honest and supportive relationships. I call these women, "Friends of Sheila". Several are already listed, but the others are Mindy Raymond Benson, Ashland Viscosi, Susanne Dejernett, Evonne Atlas, Kristin Johansen-Berg, Suzanne Weinert, Vicki Mechling, Lauren Alexander-Labahn, and Nikki Bonner.

This book would not exist without the faith and vision of Meghan Fitzpatrick, my editor, and friend. She has been present at every step of the creative process, and I am so very grateful.

Preface

"Launched in 1990, the Hubble Telescope saw nothing 'clear' until the COSTAR 'fix' in 1993. Subsequently, Hubble revealed breathtaking views of the Universe.

In 1993, I met a special physician who became a pre-eminent nephrologist and friend; he always had a kind word and a smile. The years slowly passed…then, he moved away and out of our lives.

January 2017 our paths crossed again, generating happy memories of our 'early years' and sharing patient vignettes, our medicine 'war stories'. Upon parting, he reminded me that 'Life is a marathon, not a sprint.'

That was the last time I ever saw him.

My friend called me in January 2018 to inform me that 'he' had actually been born a 'she'. She was 'transgender'. This revelation was a shock. There was disbelief but primarily a sense of grief and loss. Upon loving acceptance, and a small 'tincture of time', I recognized the intrinsic qualities that make one whole are there all along

regardless of gender. This is the 'Spirit Walker' the Native Americans speak of...

Just as Galileo was persecuted and nearly put to death by the Church for stating that the Sun circled the Earth and not the alternative...one day Society may understand that what we 'recognize' as normal is one of many amazements...just as the Hubble Telescope has revealed.

Hopefully, this book shall provide clear vision for those in need and display wonders of the world others never knew were present."

P. CARTER SNODGRASS, M.D., MBA

MATTHEW 7:1-3

Prologue

"What you are, the world is. And without transformation, there can be no transformation of the world."

—J. KRISHNAMURTI

My mentor, Dr. Brugh Joy, wrote the following in 1996: "The holy call is a revelation, an inner prompting, a vision, causing an individual to turn from a personal, self-centered, and superficially expressed life to that of a servant of the divine. The numinosity of such a transcendent call is often of such a magnitude that the individual experiences a rupture of his or her life. He or she is cast into a vaster consciousness, and often acts with the sense of extreme vulnerability and wounding brought on by the leaving behind—and therefore the betrayal of—everything that had previously held primary value in the individual's personal life. The members of the family, circle of friends, professional colleagues, and organizations threatened by such a disruption may exert extreme pressure to reform the called

one. And, failing that, to ignore or, worse yet, to cast out the 'misguided' individual. The effect of the spiritual call- to cause a transformation, of varying degrees, of both the individual and the collective-completes the divine intention."

For most of my life, I have lived within normative boundaries. As a Caucasian male growing up in a politically conservative and traditionally Christian environment, I was offered a certain implied vision of life which I accepted without great debate. It was further substantiated in my time at West Point, in the military, and in my years of practicing medicine. In this paradigm, the majority rules. Men have certain duties and responsibilities to God, country, and family. Although there are exceptions, it is a masculine dominated world. "Upstanding" people follow a well defined Christian path to earn the love and the good grace of a loving if jealous God. In this life, we are born imperfect and can find forgiveness and return to grace only through claiming Christ as savior. Other religious systems are flawed, and those believing in them are doomed. These were beliefs that I did not often articulate, but they were bedrock underlying a tribal vision. My views have shifted, radically in some cases, but I cast no stones. However, I will never again accept secular beliefs when they create polarities and support divisiveness. Despite great inertia pushing relentlessly from contrasting sides, we must look for common ground. I truly believe: love bears all things.

Like most, I have lived my life with a certain ethos. I have tried to do my best, be kind to others, follow the Golden Rule, earn a decent living, and be a good family man. I have not been anything close to perfect, but intent has been consistent. Growing up during the Civil Rights movement, I saw myself as fiscally conservative, but socially sophisticated. I believed that all are created with equal rights and fully acknowledged that there was discrimination in our culture that manifested in many forms. I felt that many of the public struggles of women, gays, and racial minorities were legitimate, but I had little time and less energy to offer to the dialogue. Although I was sympathetic, I had no compelling reason to become active in those movements.

I was also aware of stories about an emerging transgender narrative. That felt different at some level, but, again, I was too busy taking care of a large medical practice, and trying to get home each night to a family. I did not have the resources nor drive to devote to legitimate, albeit, distant causes. This was my mantra: "I just don't want to pay more taxes." In retrospect, it was a very narrow, entitled, and pejorative view of the world. That all changed in 2013.

In the spring of 2013, I had a clear revelation that I was, and always had been, a woman. This inner prompting was unanticipated yet extremely clear. Sitting in my vacation home in the idyllic West Indies, something deep within me said very plainly: "I am a woman." It was a clear message,

and with it came an imperative to do something about it. I had had similar prompts encouraging me to go to West Point and to enter medicine as a vocation. This was clearer, more forceful, and was of a much higher order of magnitude. Subsequently, I began to experience dysphoria or an uneasiness about my gender. I had an intense need to experience myself as a woman. I had had brief glimpses of this process throughout my life, but, the force and power of the feeling that presented was immense. This was a vastly alien experience, and I felt completely lost.

Over the next two years, I educated myself about gender. I cannot say with clarity what "transgender" is. It is an extremely complex condition that seemingly involves the psyche, physical body, emotions, and spirit in varying degrees. Little is reported in the medical literature. There are few studies about the long-term effects of hormones, and fewer on the possible genetic underpinnings. The bible of psychiatry, DSM-IV, classified it as a pathologic condition. Although this changed in the most recent version, there is a whole generation raised on the belief that it is a psychiatric illness.

In 2017 there were sixty-two books newly listed on Amazon about transgender issues. These speak to a variety of subjects and obstacles faced in transition, in living, and in integration of skill sets. There are now multiple feature-length films and documentaries that address the process. The take home: there is no singular transgender experience. There are thousands of variations in time of

presentation, depth of dysphoria, and in the variability of gender expression. Each individual has a unique narrative. The only common modifier is this: a distinct feeling of being uncomfortable with one's birth gender. In my own journey, the dysphoria became crippling later in life and did not dissipate until I began hormone therapy.

This inner call was not simply a physiological process. There was a spiritual underpinning to it. I certainly had dysphoria, which was a very intense physical experience, but there was something deeper that shifted in my psyche. Having been in recovery for alcohol issues for over twenty years, the spiritual terrain was not foreign to me. I had a regimen of prayer and meditation that had been rigorously developed on a daily basis over the course of decades. I had a decent grasp of what the recovery literature calls a "Higher Power". Suddenly, though, after many years of attending twelve-step meetings, sponsoring others within that venue, and following the precepts as best I could, there was a deep call to become more committed to something I can only describe as "numinous". The spiritual guides that I had become familiar with during my many years of sobriety suddenly, unexpectedly, and clearly, wanted to become more intimate. Something called to me, and I knew that I had to answer. It was that simple.

Subsequently, I have come to believe that one of my major life purposes is to use my experience and resources to help educate others about the transgender journey. I initially tried to ignore the prompt, as the media is full

of stories about transgender individuals losing family, jobs, security, and safety. It is well documented that the pressures generated by such an odd process can wreck life-long relationships, affiliations, and commitments. Despite my protestation and attempts to ignore it, the inner voice became more insistent. It was only when I let go of my resistance that I found clear evidence that from an early point in my life I had known at some level that I was a woman. The inner prompting thus was an "awakening" to something that I had been born with.

The commitment to act has created great havoc in many areas of my life. Dr. Joy's descriptive could not be more cogent. Family, friends, colleagues, and organizations have threatened me with an array of pressures. Most have been made with the intent to coerce recapitulation of my narrative or a return to my former identity. As a result, the last year has been one of disruption, confusion, and sorrow. But, in this darkness, there has been the gift of a great light. Such calling comes with blessings as well as the curses that I have suggested. Central among them is this: despite all the negative inertia and insults, I know who I am, what I am, and how I am to serve. With such clarity, each time I have been at my ego's lowest point or blinded by its small view of the world, I have been able to reorient from within. I never have felt alone nor abandoned. This certain knowledge is a beacon, and it continues to provide a daily orientation that keeps me on an authentic, if unusual, path. It has also opened in me

a great sense of compassion. I volunteer at a clinic that initiates hormonal therapy for transgender patients. I feel the pain and experience the despair of these people in ways I never could or would have before. This sensitivity makes me aware that we are all united by two universal processes: death and brokenness.

To be lost in the fog of the dramatic complexities of today's world without a true sense of self is hell. I have been there. The scores of vignettes that follow are tales from the heart. They track, through time, my unusual journey wearing many masks. I have been father, husband, paratrooper, West Pointer, physician, recovering alcoholic, and now, transgender woman. The stories speak of a human journey filled with randomness, death, sadness, failure, complexity, success, revelation, joy, and redemption. They tell the tales of common people with uncommon insight, wisdom, vigilance, and kindness. They paint a clear description of the deeper topography of a varied life to augment one point: we each tread a common road, and, all of us are just trying to get home. Clearly, many live lives tainted by silent desperation. I am coming to suspect that it is only in helping each other that we are freed from a bondage of self. I truly believe it is the primary way that we heal from the wounds of being human.

See this book for what it is: a collection of simple stories from a random life. By necessity, some names, locations, and dates have been changed to protect privacy.

This does not detract from a remarkable discovery: I have been witness to great heroism, courage, and tenacity. In reading these, I am prayerful that one gets a sense of the integrity that resonates in so many of the characters. I have had the gift of living among many brave souls. With such great teachers and with such sacred prompting can I be anything but transparent about my experience of living?

I am hopeful that the honest narratives will awaken compassion in those mystified, unsettled, and completely against all things "transgender". I am not an anomaly, not an abomination. I am a human who has lived a decent life trying to do the best that I can with what I have. I am a commoner and one among.

If we are to get past the polarities that politicize and create so much divisiveness, rancor, and hate, then we must awaken to the things that we have in common. I hope that in reading about my journey, one sees what I have seen, and feels what I have felt. Perhaps, then, my documentation of the experience of going through something completely novel can be accepted as valid and insightful. It will only be by using such technique that transformation on an individual and collective basis can be initiated. In this way, my prayer is to shine a bright light on the first step in the long journey to understanding; and, ultimately, to the dissolution of the illusion that we are alone in a fierce and random universe.

Cleaning Out the Closet

"Be patient toward all that is unsolved in your heart and try to love the questions themselves, like locked rooms and like books that are now written in a very foreign tongue. Do not now seek the answers, which cannot be given you because you would not be able to live them. And the point is, to live everything. Live the questions now. Perhaps you will then gradually, without noticing it, live along some distant day into the answer."

—RAINER MARIA RILKE

I am leaving home. I am not only leaving the house, I am leaving who I have been. What astonishing changes. I am in the midst of birthing a new me. Ready or not, I am a transgender woman awakening to the reality of who and what I am. It has certainly not been pretty. But, it is time now. Time to leave. I know it at the core of my being: Sheila Grace is growing up.

I look at my clothes and remember so many stories. The pretty blond suit I wore to work the first week so many years ago, that blue shirt to speak at Rev. Lang's funeral, the elegant dark blue suit at West Point when we gave money, the brown coat when I owed tax money and went to a beloved friend for help. There is my father's beautiful red sweater jacket. He bought that in San Diego and loved it like he loved his time there. There is the threadbare sweat top that I found in a shop the first week my oldest went to school, and the short sleeve shirt I wore my first trip to our lovely vacation place. Each has a story. I hope that when I donate them, each finds a good home. I believe those who wear them will feel the quality and blissful energy they hold and do positive things while wearing them.

My mother and father worked hard while I was growing up. He was a grocer man and she helped wherever she could. We took off Thanksgiving afternoon and Christmas, but every other day was a workday. And, each one of those days, whether the store burned down, or my grandfather died, or Kennedy was shot, or 9-11 happened, my mother and father suited up and showed up. They were that type of people.

My mother inherited a good amount of money in 1985. We all went on a trip to England. We stayed at the nicest places, and ate the best food. At Harrods, the world famous department store, my father wanted to buy me a very expensive cashmere coat. I felt so guilty that it cost

so much and said, "No thanks". He never said much about it, but I knew that hurt him. I don't know why I thought of it today while cleaning out my closet, but somehow, I wish I had let him buy it. I wish I had it to put on and to remember the day my father had the resources to do things in the world. I know now that buying that coat for me was important to him. So often, while wearing these men's clothes, I have missed the subtle lessons and the nuances of life. As a man, I have just blindly done a lot of things I wish I could change. But, I can't.

Most people in my life understand very little of this whole process. We all tend to form images of ourselves and of others, and assume that what we think is a valid and singular reality. For so long I was a West Point graduate, a physician, a devoted husband. It was the most natural thing to create a mental construct and to build a whole mythology around this narrative. I was kind, at times aggressive, but always did my best. I was an alcoholic, but after coming back from treatment, the sober years drifted by where I helped raise a family and was devoted to my mate. I was, in one of those suits, an alpha-male of the highest order. I never thought I could change nor leave. And, I almost didn't, which would have been certain death.

In the last several years, I have had to learn a great deal about who and what I was. I have had to listen to my dreams, write down and decipher my thoughts, trust my instincts, and have had to make some horribly hard choices. No one could do these things for me. They had

to be done alone. That is what truly growing up means, I guess. To fearlessly abandon the images and ideas that no longer fit.

So, standing in my closet today, I remember all the things I have been and look forward to a time when I finally feel at home in my own skin. All I can do is put on one of those pretty skirts, or the gorgeous St. John knit, and open my heart. That is what strong women do. It is sad that it took so many days in men's clothing to realize who and what I am. But, now that I have, now that I understand, I must march on like the warrior woman I always knew I was.

"Don't judge what you don't understand."

"I am astonished, disappointed, pleased with myself. I am distressed, depressed, rapturous. I am all these things at once, and cannot add up the sum. I am incapable of determining ultimate worth or worthlessness; I have no judgment about myself and my life. There is nothing I am quite sure about. I have no definite convictions—not about anything, really. I know only that I was born and exist, and it seems to me that I have been carried along. I exist on the foundation or something I do not know."

—CARL JUNG

It is Thanksgiving 2017. I am in the West Indies. It is a paradise of sights, sounds, and feels so sweet. There is such a softness inherent in all possible things: the gentle blue ocean, the smooth green rolling mountains,

the puffy cotton clouds, the solid natives, the constant of an ebb-flow of tide; the peace. I am at a place in my life where I seek to gather myself. I feel stuck. I look back and seek to discern some pattern in the massive forces that are at work. So much is going on. I ponder and think, as that is what I am used to. Surely I can find my way through this! But, Jung's unrelentingly honest descriptive is what I grapple with. Although the dreams seem to come with more intent and there is a hope that coats all thinking with a sheen that makes things bright and lucid, something is missing. "There is nothing I am sure about." That says it all.

I have lost a sense of my bearings. For so long my job, family, and reputation gave me some points of reference. No longer. My family is not here. We are not the single unit I thought we were. We are spread and pulled apart in a litany of ways. What does that mean? I look at a picture of us on safari. I had just retired after selling my medical practice for a large amount of money. There I am in khaki safari gear, seated with legs crossed and a hat set at a jaunty angle, looking like a smug Indiana Jones. My family surrounding me, all in white. Each of us has a glow. We have money in the bank, our bright futures loom, and we are together. God, it seemed so perfect. From a certain perspective, I judge it as one of the best moments of my life. So much has seemingly changed, and like Jung, "I cannot add up the sum."

A relative called me earlier to wish me a good holiday.

They say as they are hanging up, "I hope you find yourself." I immediately become self-critical, and the tapes start to play in my head: "I should never have pursued this transgender process. How selfish, how crazy, how pathetic." Sadness and shame appear from the shadows. For, in all honesty, I miss the steady, masculine, soldering soul that so easily mapped out complex plans with accuracy. I miss having reasoned answers, and being "right". I miss not being sure of myself and the boldness that gave reassurance about a particular future and outcome. I miss the Indiana Jones father that had such keen judgment and insight. Where is he?

Jerelle was a patient in my practice. He was twenty-something and missed dialysis treatments with frequency. In my arrogance, I assumed that it meant that he did not value his life nor appreciate the care. I was quick to judge. Despite the drama that played out between us, there was an odd friendship that we constructed over several years. One day when I had been on his case about his diet and lack of self-care, he said to me, "Doc, you don't know nothing about my life. I hitch a ride or walk home, but I'm always sick after four hours on this damn machine. I got no family and do day labor when I have the strength. I sell drugs, steal, and do whatever I can just to live. I can't afford the food or medicine you want for me. I'm poor, black, sick, and that ain't changing. That's just the way it is. I'm stuck. Don't judge what you don't understand."

Sometime later, Jerelle came to the Emergency Room

in a coma. I assumed that it was a drug overdose, but that was not the case. It turned out that he had an inflammatory condition that shut down his brain and central nervous system. The underlying process was never clear, but it required constant vigil, a gamut of unusual medications, and daily dialysis. Several times I gave up on him, but each time, he would rally. During four long weeks, he did not rouse. The nurses that took care of him turned him religiously so that he wouldn't get pressure sores. The consultants that came gave their best. No king could have received better care; and, one day he woke up. When the nurse called to tell me, I cried like a child. When I saw him awake, I hugged him. "Where have you been?", I asked. Jerelle just grinned and said, "I don't know, but it's ok Doc. It is all ok." From that point, I cannot say that my friend became the model patient, but, there was a new softness that I cannot describe. Something in that month-long walk in another realm created a shift at some deep level. Whatever had occurred, Jerelle was lighter and more at peace. He was quicker to smile. He was less anxious. He found some level of acceptance.

Sometime after I left the practice, Jerelle died. I have thought about him today as I sit here watching the palms shiver, and the gentle waves lap peacefully in the turquoise vista sat just before me. I felt first the sadness that Jerelle tried to convey and carried for both of us. The imperious sentence of race, gender, creed, and genetics. I then felt the anxiousness that he wore like a coat. The hell our mind

and ego generate from value judgments about each and every thing human. I then sensed the hopelessness that riddled his thoughts most days. How could such a dismal journey have any redemption? It sat with me like a dark cloud. But, later in the day, I suddenly thought of him again. That smile he brought out of the coma. I caught a glimpse of the peace that came with the awakening. Something unspeakable happened to Jerelle, and I was witness to it.

I wish above many things that I could sit and talk with him right now. First, I would listen with intent. Then, I would tell him "thank you" from the depths of my soul. I see now the courage and conviction with which he walked his days. He was no saint, but he was authentic and did what he could in the best ways he knew how. He took the things that came, made do the best he knew how, and awoke one day unfettered by his own judgments about what was or was not. He waited and stayed afloat and when all seemed lost, came to that most peaceful of places that Jung speaks to: "Where there is no judgment about myself and my life." I witnessed a miracle.

This Thanksgiving Day, he whispers to me through the curtains of time and space. With a beautiful and peaceful smile, he finds me in some remarkable way and whispers, "Doc, don't judge. You got to remember that. Don't judge. It's all okay, just the way it is. Perfect. Just the way it is." I see now, looking back, how rare in life it is to be comfortable in one's own shoes. I see how utterly remarkable it is

in the desperation of day to day that so many experience that we ever get a sense of peace and a feeling that things are good, right, well lighted, and clean. However he got it, I am glad that my friend received grace and comfort in that time and in that way. And, in doing that, the most remarkable of things happened: he passed it on to me. I can only aspire to do the same.

"Please let me see my husband."

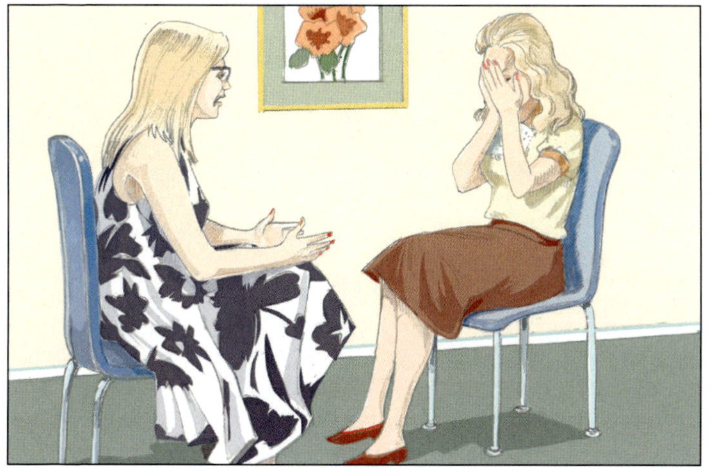

"If you bring forth what is within you, what you bring forth will save you. If you do not bring forth what is within you, what you do not bring forth will destroy you."

—GOSPEL OF THOMAS

It is late Thursday afternoon on a warm October day. I am going in to see a new patient and her significant other at Kind Clinic. I do volunteer work here and it has been a long and exhausting day, but this couple has driven several hours to be here. As well, they have waited months for the appointment. I take a breath and open the door. As I step in, there is a heated exchange going on between two women, one well-dressed and transgender, the other, distinguished and cis-gender. The latter is in tears, but as I introduced myself and sit, the last part of the exchange that I hear while walking in still rings in my ears: "Where is my husband?" Before I can even finish introducing myself, the cis-gender woman screams at her partner: "Please take off that wig, and the make-up. I want to see my husband. I miss him so very, very much. I need him, I miss him. Please." The transgender woman tries to console her, and says quietly, "Sweetie, we have been all through this. It is me in here. I am the same person that has been married to you for over thirty years." The other woman will not relent and now, sobbing, says this: "No, I know he is in there. You are *not* the same. I want my husband. Please, please." This is purgatory for both. Sadly, it is not the first time I have seen such a gut-wrenching exchange.

Many years prior, it is past midnight, and I sit in front of a nine-year-old African-American boy. He has come to the hospital with his father who is gravely ill. The father has severe, chronic diabetes and is admitted with chest

pain. There was no other family, and the father took good care of the boy. By what I could see, where one went, the other followed. They were bound at a sacred level. At nine years of age, a good father can do no wrong. Solid, present, protective, loving, kind, he holds the answers to all great and small questions.

Something goes terribly wrong. The father clutches his chest and calls the nurse before passing out. The boy is hustled out to the conference room. He hears the crescendo of orders and the chaos of nurses and doctors trying with electric paddles and strong medicine to revive the most important person in all the world: his father.

Things do not go well. I am there, and since I am the attending doctor, the duty to inform the son falls to me. The young boy fights and twists, "When can I see my father?" he asks. I take a deep breath. "Listen," I say, "I am so sorry to tell you that your father has passed away." He looks at me. He is stunned and lost and looking for something, anything, to hang on to. "What do you mean?" He is pleading. "I need my Dad. Please let me see my Dad," he cries. It is the same gut-wrenching, never-can-be-the-same, voice that I heard then and I hear it again now.

Deep and pain-filled tears flow as I drive away from the Clinic. I am going through a similar transition and the exchange between the patient and her wife hits close to home. I cannot find peace. I play the conversation back in my heart. This is such new, unplowed ground for many of us. There are no maps to follow, no guides. The people

whom I know and trust from Alcoholics Anonymous and long-term friendships are gentle and kind, but they have seen nothing like this. There is no fluency in the language of the heart that can be a salve for such odd and sad experiences. I think back and wonder what became of the nine-year-old? Losing one's father from a heart attack at such a young age has edges and searing pain. But, the cruel death and life that follow are reconcilable in the heart and head. Some solid relative steps forward and a circle of care eases the pain. The boy grows up to become a man with deep, but healed scars. But, the transgender experience involves much deeper currents and issues. The complexities of gender, marriage, values, cultural expectations all conspire to make it a brutal arena for people transitioning and those that have loved and depended on them.

"Please let me see my husband." The words sit like a boulder on my chest. What right do I have to shed the mask I have worn to become a woman? How can I reconcile this?

I heard a story on the radio many years ago. A married woman with a large family and a man married to someone else run away together. They never look back and never make amends. They just up and leave. When I heard it, I thought about how the children left behind must have been devastated by such a thing. How sad, the tears and loss of losing a parent or spouse in this chthonic way.

Today, I remember the story but think more now about what the woman must have felt. How driven she must have been to flee the ties that bind one to a mate and children

in such a deep way. She must have come to a dark place where she felt pulled, drained by family and fortune, and was dying. She must have seen one chance to redeem the one life she had some control over. Her own.

I can relate to that. I have known for a long time that something was calling to me. The day that I moved out to my own space and became a woman full-time, I did so in desperation. I could die in place or move. If we are human, we feel and grieve this in the deepest way. I hate the explosive pain that such a move fosters. It generates such fear and darkness. Not only in me, but in my family. I hate that so very much, but I cannot forget the dysphoria and the insistent urging that I had from within to live an authentic life. I was at a crossroads and bifurcations of this nature have one rule: make a choice.

I think we each have a defining moment, where we take all that we are and all that we know and feel, and make that one decision. We can look back and hope it turns out right, but, by nature, it is destructive. Lives and loves are butchered in the blink of an eye. The real truth is this: it is only by having the courage to feel that pain and to move into the raw space that follows, that we find true redemption and growth. I may be wrong about all of this, but in my deepest parts, I think making that decision is the apex of a life. Everything else is fluff. It is the one and only thing that we are truly responsible for.

"Cause, that is just the way it is."

> *"We can't become what we need to be by remaining what we are."*
>
> —ANONYMOUS

I am walking the Jacqueline Onassis Reservoir in Central Park. I have come to see Rick Linklater's new film premier and to be with friends. I am here as my transgender self, Sheila Grace. This is the first time I have been out in public as a woman in a place other than my hometown. It marks such a time of transition in my life and in all my relationships. Am I ready?

The sky softens to a light grey, and the blustery wind turns cool. It is late-fall, and I know in weeks there will be frost. Stark winter looms in the dark. Change is at hand. The gulls dip and dive into the deep, black water, and I

feel shifting down in my bones. As a doctor, I have borne witness to such massive flux in the lives of others; to see it, and to feel it, erupting in mine, is odd.

Carol was in her sixties when I became her doctor. I loved her and her grumpy, old, gnarled husband from the start. Once she required dialysis three times a week, gumming his Beechwood chew, Dan would drive her over from their hometown which was a hundred miles away. I would sometimes see him holding her tight to get her large body out of the car, or gently clutching her arm as he pried her out of the wheelchair. She would grunt and groan and cuss like a sailor. He would smile and kiss her on the forehead. It was a dance, and he always followed her lead. As Carol fought on, she had small stroke-lets that caused her a progressive and deep confusion. It frustrated her that she could not think nor remember. But, she tried her best. Later, she could not remember my name, so she just called me "George". When I asked why that particular name, she just hunched her shoulders and said, "Cause, that's just the way it is." And, that was the truth at so many levels.

I believe that we are fundamentally selfish by nature. The big shifts, living, dying, and the seismic alterations of relationships that dot our lives, affect others with their bite and bluster. However, despite the drama that we foster within the world, these are things we do alone. Movements of consequence are done in the dark. If we are blind to the actions, then the reactions of those close to us may

be the one and only mirror we have. Both Dan and Carol took the ravaging of disease as something natural, and not something to fight. But, I could see the sadness in the old man as his wife changed to a shell of the complex being who had trooped with him for over fifty years. It was no one's fault, but it was sad and relentless; and, above all, intensely personal.

Later, I am at a stylish restaurant. I have full makeup on and am waiting for my friend to come back from the women's room. I begin to think how I would have felt seeing my father go through such a radical change. His life and my relationship to both he and my mother were loving. However, they were stilted and stuffy affairs. I never thought of judging what I saw, nor really bothered to form an opinion. They were my parents and, like actors on the screen, or mythological creatures, they did things that I would later reflect on, but never felt close to touching.

But, I am faced with something different. This life alteration, like that of Carol to her devoted husband, is something up-close and personal. There are subtle, yet dramatic changes that are magnified. And, these shifts have edges that cut and bruise the consciousness of those closest to us. Whatever I may think, the effect of my choices, however reasoned or not, is palpable. They stir emotions and demand judgment. Spoken or unspoken, there are fluxes in intimate places with my friends and kin that cause riptides that rankle like the gulls diving beneath the surface of the Reservoir water.

When I saw my mother's body just after she had died, it was as if I was seeing her for the first time. The reality of her life and her movements in my life over decades struck me with a force that I still feel. Why did it take such a long time to dive into that relationship, and to experience the richness that she wanted to create?

I was afraid, but the younger transgender women I see in my volunteer work seem so much braver. They seem far beyond me in maturation and willing to watch and move with the fluxes in life which augment such odd currents. I could, I think, at some earlier point in this whole process, have just shoved it down into the dark and lived out a life of sorts. It would not have been authentic, but would have been consistent and predictable, like those of my parents. I have no idea what the things I am doing will do to the interior lives of those closest to me. But, as my friend and I flirt with a waiter, it strikes me that with all the change, all the shifting, and all the discomfort, we all will survive. Growth is optional.

I am wishful that in the dark places that we accommodate such things, the love that binds will somehow resonate and shine through like the sun bursting through the clouds on that fall afternoon during my walk in Central Park. I hope that in the end we will all do our own inner work, and hug each in whatever form we are manifesting. Why? Because, as Carol intimated, *that is how life is*, it is how we grow. The epitaph for us all: "Cause, that is just the way it is."

Small and Fragile Mysteries

"As far as we can discern, the sole purpose of human existence is to kindle a light in the darkness of mere being."

—CARL JUNG

I have long struggled with finding my truth in this life. But, in such restlessness, there has been the gift of occasional insight. I find the following in an old journal: "So very many people, each with a destiny, each with a set of fears and hopes. The world in such setting appears so random. That makes the love and goodwill that spring through the cracks in the blistering indifference so very remarkable. I am refinding my belief, that the world is such a large venue, but is played out in such small and fragile mysteries."

It is late. I am still in process, but I continue to grapple. As I do so, I believe even more deeply now what I wrote then. There is a tenacity that has appeared while living

my way into this "fragile mystery". I am not interested in fluff; I want truth. I am motivated by only one question: how does one lead an authentic life?

This one life is all I have, so it is not an esoteric exercise. Everywhere, I see people like me, desperate to find some meaning, some relevance. My experiences make me ever more interested in the mechanics and underpinnings that authenticity is built upon. There seems to be one common feature that I continue to find in the lives of those who have lived in such a way. It is a phenomenon named "calling".

Vincent Van Gogh once said: "Your profession is not what brings home your weekly paycheck, your profession is what you're put here on earth to do, with such passion and such intensity that it becomes spiritual in calling."

Oprah, the Black Madonna of our times, says this: "I believe there's a calling for all of us. I know that every human being has value and purpose. The real work of our lives is to become aware. And awakened. To answer the call."

The modifiers of passion and intensity seem to appear, along with trust, in most lives that honor true callings. The spiritual aspect is more ephemeral, but I suspect it is central to everything else. I am beginning to remember that a true calling has at its core, a tie with something greater. Callings bind us to the Sacred in some inexplicable way. Callings lead us home.

I think of the stories and people in my journey that

have suggested what this all looks like. I remain constantly fascinated by the life of Joan d'Arc. However one tries to explain the phenomena that was this young woman's life, it leads to a larger and larger mystery. How does an illiterate teenage girl from the hinterland mobilize, and lead to victory, a French army beaten down by a hundred years of English power and might? There is no rational way to explain it. Somehow, in some mystical way, Something intervened in the affairs of man and, through a sense of calling, orchestrated something magical.

Is this an anomaly? I don't think so. Although not as notorious as that of Joan, there are personal experiences that show me that lives can be directed toward authenticity by listening to a call. W.B., my therapist for many years, is one of them. Early in our journey together, I learn that she began her training much later in life than is the norm. It is not until she nears her fortieth birthday that she leaves the comforts of her home to move to Zurich. She speaks no German, French or Flemish. She knows almost no one when she lands in Switzerland. Thousands of miles away, she has left a family unit with children in school, a husband, a paying job, a good reputation. What is the genesis of such a radical later-in-life shift? Why does she feel so compelled to do something that, despite support, shakes her family to the core? The first time I ask, she says with a quirky grin: "Simple, it was my calling."

There seem to be characteristics that are common to real calling. First, they appear, when honored, to hold

great power. During the first several years that I meet with W.B., she listens with intent during my shining and whining moments. She is present in so many ways during a time that I feel something coming to the surface. I have no experience in this realm, so she stays the course with me. She guides me through a maze of confusion and doubt. Week after week I talk about my restlessness and feelings of dis-ease. I detail the dreams pointing to something wanting to arise which I will not or cannot verbalize. I labor on, and, she, ever the wise guide, lets me stumble along. She frames the issues and reflects back what I say, and don't say. She gives great insight through her own experience. But, true to her art: she gives no answers. She reminds me chronically that it is my struggling and exploration alone that lead to clarity. She teaches me the recipe for most truth: thesis, antithesis, synthesis. It is only in retrospect that I see that her honoring her own call has fostered a fluency with an integrity. It is this integrity that guides her, and in a mysterious way, it guides me also.

Second, as I move deeper into an exploration of my personal journey, I realize that callings happen frequently. They are not uncommon, although they may be difficult to hear. Biblically speaking, "many are called." They happen at different times in the life journey and under different circumstances. They spring from a legion of sources: from dreams, from rituals, from religion, from mentors, from books. However different they may appear, most of us have places in our lives where we feel inexplicably drawn

to something that is impossible to explain to others. Dante describes the angst in *The Divine Comedy*: "In the middle of the road of my life I awoke in a dark wood, where the true way was wholly lost."

For years, despite the scores of hour-long exchanges, I sometimes leave my therapy sessions thinking how lost I feel. Then one day, I have an epiphany. As a transgender woman, I am being called to transition. Think about the people you know: an uncle that "went off to war," the sister that becomes a nun, the aunt that "ran away" to live as a starving artist in Paris, the brother that divorces a woman and marries a man. These are all life choices that seem to have at their core a sense of being directed to someone or to something. These are callings in the truest sense.

Third, they are intensely personal. It is often not easy to understand another's calling. I can fathom little about the motives behind most of these decisions in the lives of others. So frequently, they just make no sense. As odd as it sounds, it is not until I begin my own exploration of being transgender that I come to fully comprehend this.

In my family, my great-grandfather Morton, whose own great-grandfather had signed the Declaration of Independence, is an itinerant Methodist preacher. He rides horseback to "share the word" in small West Texas outbacks like Notrees and Vealmoor. He is dirt poor and has five bright girls and a skeptical wife to feed. Why such an odd and demanding journey? All because he, "heard the call." My paternal grandfather, Jack, is eigh-

teen when he enlists in the service. In his hometown, a red bi-plane drops out of a shiny blue July sky. He hugs his mother and jumps aboard to be swept away. He is one of the first enlisted pilots in the Army Air Corps. Not given to too many words, he says years later: "I just felt a calling. It was what I had to do." My beloved maternal grandmother, Martha, begins to paint with acrylics after fifty. I still have some of her work. It is not auction grade, but there is a savage beauty and real passion that slashes through in distinctive color and style. When I ask her why she started to paint, she just says, "I don't know, it was just something I knew I had to do."

Fourth, we oppose what we do not understand. Sadly, it is often those closest to us that hurt us the most in this way. Culturally, we are prone to diminish, often savagely, those who have committed to a calling. I can still hear my mother with a sharp and condescending voice saying about a neighbor who publicly devotes his life to a cause she finds fault with, "Oh, he is such a silly little man."

I see many transgender patients in clinic each week. Each carries the scars of abuse and ridicule from others who distort this process into something dangerous or immoral. It is neither, but it suggests that opposition is often the price of awakening to a calling. Such opposing inertia, though, creates something the Greeks called "metis". They prized this attribute above most everything. It was that quality of being that was linked to the Sacred, as it was the guiding force behind all true unfolding. More

reliable than thought, more palpable than dreams, more spontaneous than doing, it is a sense of the divine that blossoms ever more densely as the calling is honored. Linked in this way to the mystery within, when I become unsure, or afraid, if I will but sit and allow the mind to settle, the right action invariably arises unprompted. That is metis. This Force that we are linked to in such a way can never be untrue to itself.

Fifth, failure to honor one's own calling has consequences. I am learning that callings uniquely lead us to the places where we grow. I sense that we are built to be ripped open and to lose whatever limited sense of what we think we are. This human journey is so full of light, yet so married to the dark. But, it is by being willing to accept the call that we are led, finally, to who and what we really are. If I ignore it, I become lost in my own fragile theatrics and see only what my ego fashions. By honoring the call, we do not magically become rich or famous, but more importantly, we uncover the true reality: we are both human and divine.

Coming To the Bones

"There is a pain-so utter-
That it swallows substance up-
Then covers the Abyss with Trance-
So Memory can step
Around-across-upon it-
As one within a Swoon-
Goes safely-where an open eye-
Would drop him- Bone by bone."

—EMILY DICKINSON

In the early years of my medical practice, I had a patient who was deaf and mute. She also had kidney failure from the ravages of her fulminant and inherited diabetes mellitus. She was on dialysis. And, if all that were not enough, she had also lost her sight. She was blind.

She spent her days traveling the country giving talks to a variety of large groups. Blind, deaf, mute, diabetic,

and a dialysis patient, this incredible woman was also a motivational speaker. Really. One of her sisters would speak for her as she signed. Her message was simple: "One can never see the bigger picture. Just do what you can with what you have, and always be grateful." By report, she received standing ovations and rave reviews wherever she went.

I remember the night that she died. As I drive to the Emergency Room where she had been transported after a massive heart attack, I wonder how I can console the family. There will be such deep grief. As I walk into the room, the family is there hovering over her now dead body. There is a reverence, but no wailing, no passionate cries. I am the first to break down and sob as I see her dead body. The sisters, whom I had come to know well, console *me*.

These were religious people. As we hold hands and they recite prayers, there is a deep peace that fills the room. I am still mired in my addiction, and years away from going to treatment, but, despite the wall around my heart, I can feel the love and comfort. As I am leaving, one of the sisters stops me, gives me a hug, and says, "Don't be sad, there is a bigger story here. There is so much that we are blind to, but my sister is in a place now where she understands everything. Be patient. We pray for you." Her sister had just died, and she is reminding me that there is a larger process that unveils itself in its own time and that patience is vital to understanding.

It is the end of May 2017. I have announced to family

that I am transgender. None of us is really certain of anything from here. There is fear, mostly, and anger, and guilt, and chaos. In one exchange, an older family member asks me this question: "What's this about you being a woman?" She stands as a representative for a lot of others. This is virgin terrain for my extended clan. It is not a conversation that I could have anticipated even weeks before. But, it comes as my role as husband and father to foster a series of sinking-vessel-dialogues about this whole transgender journey. It is alien, and no one understands.

So how do I answer? First, I say that I know something certain: "I have always been like this." I speak about the way I felt while wearing make-up as a first grader in a dance recital. "The ebb and flow of the dysphoria or the discomfort I feel in not being a woman is like wanting a drink, and not getting one." I then say, "Watch the documentary *Lady Valor.* It is the saga of a Navy Seal, Kristin Beck, and her transition". I continue on, "I was suicidal for a period of time. I had a specific plan to kill myself." They lean forward and grimace in horror. "The estrogen therapy literally saved my life. It helps me feel normal. Whatever that is." I launch into a description of the difficulty in trying to negotiate this, knowing it is certain to wreck my primary relationships. I am acutely aware of the back drafts, and how messy and dark this all seems and looks. I then detail how it feels working the steps of AA on this process. I have used all the tools I can muster. This is not a character defect. I repeat the only thing I

really know for certain: "This is who I am, this is what I am, and I think I know how I am to serve this experience." Whether this can be grasped, it is the undeniable reality of where I am. After long years of feeling "something" not right in my being, I am given a truth. I am a transgender woman in the middle of a bloody and public process of transition that few seem able or willing to understand.

I represent an anomaly in the minds of many. I am neither yin nor yang in a world that longs for some immutable certainty. A land where the majority demands to know whether anything and everything is black or white. Shades of grey are seen as irrelevant or enemy, or both. It must be one or the other. In this time of questions about every form of boundary and authority, gender definition and certainty has become a conservative enclave to protect at all costs.

This is my point: we are all adrift in an ocean of seething uncertainty. Quantum mechanics now shows us that there is no certainty. We are all packets of energy, with little that is solid about us. We are in constant disequilibrium. Sometimes we are "this" and other times "that". That is the new reality. We are all migrants on an uncharted journey between the polarities of birth and death. In between, the gender choice now is obviously more fluid than what we once thought. And everything else is too!

So here I am: a staunch West Point graduate, from the heartland. I am a soldier and doctor for god's sake. I

should be one of the ones counted on and depended upon in such a time of shifting! But what irony: I am one of the ones chosen in some way to model the very process that generates the most fear and loathing. I stand as a living paradox: seemingly one thing, I am something else.

Jung speaks to this paradox when he says: "Being a part, man cannot grasp the whole. He is at its mercy. He may assent to it, or rebel against it; but he is always caught up by it and enclosed within it. He is dependent upon it and sustained by it. Love is his light and his darkness, whose end he cannot see."

So, the message that my dead, deaf, blind, and mute patient sends back to me resonates clearly: "One can never see the bigger picture from this limited human perspective." So I will be patient. It is all that can be done. I will soldier on, continue to live into the process, educate where I can, confess my ignorance and imperfection, and hope that in the end, we find, as I suspect: black and white are not opposites, they are not an abomination, they are: secret lovers.

"Push, Babe, push!"

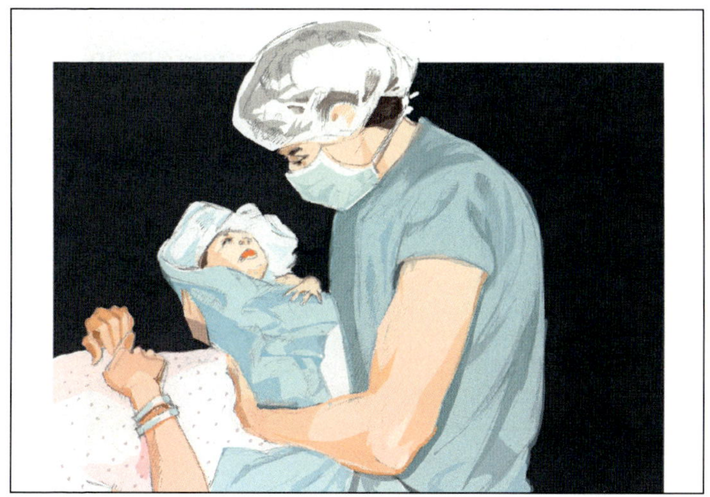

"As we are liberated from our own fear, our presence automatically liberates others."

—NELSON MANDELA

My life, with such gargantuan flux and change, seems so random just now. I cannot diminish the importance of this transition I am in: it is a huge passage. No one has a map for this sort of journey. The topography of this alien emotional landscape is varied and brutal. There are scores of peaks and valleys that must be negotiated one step by careful step. One unconscious move can be fatal. Raw with emotion and fear, I am slowly finding a rhythm. It is not pretty, but I am hopeful that I will come out on the other side with my integrity intact; and, having weathered such a storm, provide some help to many others. But, this is in the future, and just now, nothing is certain. Transitions are such fragile times.

I have spent a lifetime bearing witness to and participating in life transitions, my own and others. It is what I do. To wit, it is early on a November morning in 2002. I am the physician in my group making rounds at the hospital. I have two dozen very ill people to see. It is just the beginning of the dark days of winter when so many of my dialysis patients hit a wall and succumb to pulmonary or infectious assaults. Two of my favorite people are on my list: Joe comes from my hometown, and I dearly love him and his wife. Delbert is patriarch of a lovely family. I am the primary doctor for him and many of his tribe.

One of the nurses pokes her head around the partition where I am reviewing charts. "Doc, Delbert doesn't look good," she says in an urgent tone. He has been on dialysis for over a year. He comes to me with advanced

kidney damage from high blood pressure. It is early that we find that he has a primary kidney cancer that has already moved to his lungs. He has the kidney removed, but it puts a heavy burden on the remaining organ. The cancer, always a concern, fortunately is slow growing. After starting dialysis treatments, he has time to spend with his beloved Patty and to watch the kids grow. I see him on treatment days, and we both laugh at his corny jokes or mine. He has a lovely smile and tells me more than once that he appreciates me. That sort of bonding does not happen easily with tough men like Delbert. We both know that.

In the hospital room, it is dark, but there is enough filtered light from the window for me to see that his wife looks beat. Delbert is wan, and his respirations are shallow and raspy. He is dying. It is a dance that I know too well. There is nothing to do but hold hands and let this play out. We do. At the very end, he opens his eyes and sees us standing by the bed. We are his team. We are the people that he has grown to love and depend upon. I am there to see him across, and he knows it. He smiles as he closes his eyes for the last time. I hug his wife, wipe away the tears, and walk out.

As I step into the hall, the Charge Nurse hollers, "Doc, come down here!" As I open the door, there is Joe: he is in distress. The chronically ill are never a picture of health, but Joe has always been a fighter. His admission to the hospital this time is for something that I think will quickly

pass. Truth be known, it is really just a time for him to get some medication, and his good wife to have some rest. But, like so many other points in my life, I cannot see the larger picture. It is Joe's time to die as well. He begins to breathe deeply and heavily. His wife looks at me, and we both just shake our heads. In the midst of sadness and tears, we do what we can for Joe, and comfort each other. In the blink of an eye, he slips away.

I sit in tears at the nurse's station trying to piece together what I have just seen. As I dictate the death summaries of these two men, I am terribly sad. These are good men who have done what they were asked to do, have lived solid lives, have died with grace and dignity. They leave legacies of love with adoring families. I have been witness to the ending of two authentic lives.

I remember being present during a difficult delivery years before. The woman is term and at the point of delivery, but descent down the birth canal is stalled. Her husband is there at her side, he screams: "Push, Babe, push!" She is exhausted and can barely hear him. She cries and screams. Finally, out comes a beautiful baby girl. I have a picture in my mind of the father holding his child for the first time. Her eyes are fully open and her little hands spread wide from the shock and fear of having been dragged out of the comfort and peace of that dark, gestational cave, so full of love. The father has on a mask and has large, hairy arms. The wife is deathly exhausted. But there, for the first time are the three of them. They

are now bound forever. The child, full of adrenaline and unimagined new stimuli, is overwhelmed. She is now in a new domain. The physical world is a place of consequence, drama, and most novel, involves others. She screams, "What in the world?" Her dad senses the sacred moment, but, is full of his own fear. "How do I do this? How do I lead this woman through all of the trauma and pain life brings?" The wife, exhausted to the extreme, is full of endorphins that nature bestows on women in labor. She is flush with a blushing love, but it is tainted by activation of a mothering instinct now active: "What a miracle, but what do I do now?" Dragged into something seemingly so foreign and so very random, the three share this boundary crossing into the living realm. Forever, they are bonded by these things: fear, karma, and love.

I do not know why I have had the honor to bear witness to such transitions. But, whether it is the birth of a child, the deaths of two precious humans, or a unique bifurcation point in my own journey, I am just now beginning to accurately appreciate these events for what they are: boundary passages. They are built into the human journey. In many ways, they *are* the journey. They are the division edges of a topography that define our lives. They are not unidimensional but holographic in that they carry the essence of so much data: who, what, when, where, why. Those common passage points are, like our dreams, full of such complex substance that informs us of so much about the wider implications of our lives.

I am beginning to suspect this: we are all so magnificent, and yet, we are so tortured by a sense of being small. The signposts I pass-by in my day to days of farting and feeling alone are written in an alien language that I have assumed is hostile. Why can't I see the reality? We each are bearing witness to one another. The signposts all have one message: "You are immortal. Open your eyes and enjoy the ride."

Instead of the joy of my graduation from medical school, I remember the fear of not being enough. I choose to remember the pimple on my face on my wedding day, instead of the splendor of that beautiful ritual. I easily recall the one hateful thing my mother ever said to me in a lifetime of supportive love.

I am being called, I think, to move fully into the present tense in order to be fully available to the reality of what is. I have listened for too long to the mocking and dread of my tiny ego, which thinks we all are aimlessly adrift in a vast ocean. In my little world, I think: "I am alone." But, there are times I have been opened to the core by participating in the deep rituals of other lives. At those times, I know I am connected to Something I can only begin to imagine, and in ways I can barely fathom. The massive implications of these glimpses into the vastness of it all, fill me first with fear. But the fear is fuel. I know that I can convert it to energy, and use it to generate alertness, action, and authentic living. Delbert, Joe, and many others, all whisper together: "Push, Babe, push!"

The Price for Being Picked

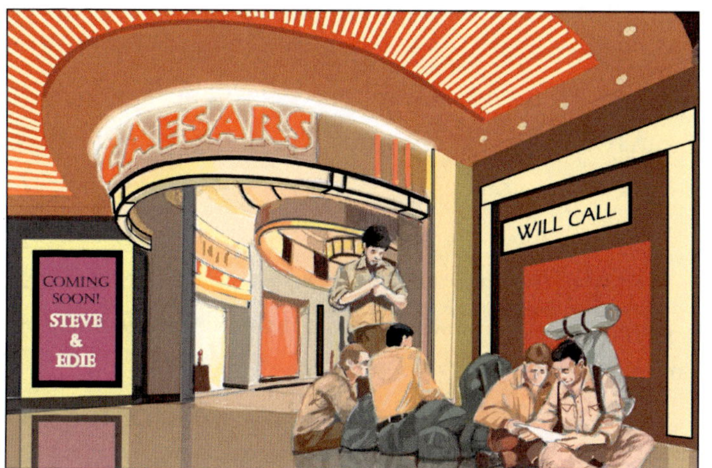

Out beyond ideas of wrongdoing
and right doing there is a field.
I'll meet you there.
When the soul lies down in that grass
the world is too full to talk about.

—RUMI

A pilgrim is a traveler who journeys to a holy place. Pilgrimage is the aspiration of travel made manifest. Seen in a certain way, we are all of us on a migratory adventure between birth and death. It takes me many years to awaken to this process. Some traditions suggest that once awake, a pilgrim is called to make a trip to a special place. It is an act of homage, usually involving sacrifice in varying degrees, and, necessitates intent. It may bolster a belief, provide an answer to an issue, or induce a change. Whatever the destination or reason, it is never, ever, to be taken lightly.

My first such experience begins Good Friday, 1998. I am with ten others. We are a diverse group, ages ranging from twenty-six to sixty-two. We come from all walks of life. We have representation from the corporate, medicine, and art worlds. One of us is retired, another in-between work. We vary in sexual preferences. I am not yet fully awake to gender issues, but that dwells in the mix. We are at Caesars Palace in Las Vegas. It is a giant festival of an evening. The Lenten season, a time of deprival in the Christian tradition, is ending. People are here to party. We are a group apart. Each of us is dressed in hiking clothes and heavy boots. We all carry a large backpack.

We eat our last commercial meal for two weeks in a fashionable Asian restaurant and in file walk to the steps on the east side of the hotel. This puts us squarely in the path of the casino. All about us are the opulence, the splendor, the intrigue of our times. But, we are a singular crew.

We will pile into a mishmash of old vans and head southwest toward the Mojave. Deep in the night, we will sleep in the dirt. As we survive the looks and laughs and finally get to the doors, from far back in the room, I hear a loud, intoxicated voice: "Save the whales. Motherfuckers, just save the whales!" I am officially on pilgrimage.

I sit on my pack and look at the full moon as we wait for Sedona Cahill and her helpers to pick us up. She will lead us on this journey into the desert. Walking up the steps are people in suits, tuxedos, formal dresses, miniskirts. A festive night in the most festive of places, and I am about to go sleep on the ground. I panic. My mind races and I think, "I've made a mistake. What in the holy hell am I doing here? I am never home as it is, and I've taken two weeks of precious vacation time to do *this?* Here I am in army garb, sitting outside of Caesars on a holiday night with people I don't even know!"

But, I take deep breaths and sit. I am reminded that beginnings are such fragile times. This is my first vision quest, a form of pilgrimage. I am an innocent, a novice. I am the Fool-Child. Nothing that I have done can nor will prepare me for the changes that it will create. None of us in this odd band will know each other before we head out into the dark night. But, for some reason, each of us has listened to a calling. We all have signed up for this adventure sponsored by Noetic Sciences, a company founded by Edgar Mitchell, the astronaut. Dedicated to exploration of consciousness in humans, we as a group, and as

individuals, represent the embodiment of the mission. Like man has done for millennia, unified by something unexplainable, we are bound by three things: wanderlust, naïveté, and courage.

We drive for several hours. We stop, get our gear. Sedona says, "Welcome to the desert. Get some rest." During the middle of the night I get up to urinate. Sleeping bags are scattered like lumpy sacks of potatoes, the night air is cool, and the fullest of moons is just overhead. It is clear as day. Suddenly, I know: I am in the right place at the right time with the right people. It is my first gift from the Universe.

With morning light, we drive to Shoshone. We are ninety miles from Las Vegas. We stop. We get busy filling the scores of gallon jugs with water that are in the back of the vans. We will drink what we bring with us. It is the first time that I feel a part of this group. In a short time, we have unbeknownst become a tribe. We head north, then west. We drive for a short distance on Jubilee Pass Road. In the middle of nowhere, we turn left off the highway onto an unmarked dirt road. We crest a small berm and park. This is our home for the next two weeks.

We are on the southern boundary of Death Valley National Park. It is the High Desert. The name comes from its elevation, and we are near four thousand feet here. To the south, the Colorado Desert and flatlands fall below sea level. The plant community is hardy with deep-rooted and salt tolerant growth. The vegetation tends to have

succulent leaves and flowers that burst with fragrance and color with any moisture. The average rainfall is only a dozen inches a year, but this is the season for unexpected downpour, depending on Pacific weather patterns. The wind is a constant. There is a small mountain that juts up a mile or so to the south. The shaggy range is the remnant of volcano activity from eons past. To the north is desert floor and the high Sierras stretch out as far as the eye can see. We are in an ancient land.

We have arrived, and make camp in the flatlands and ravines. A few cars pass on the desolate highway. The next several days we have group meetings. Each of us shares a narrative about what we think has brought us here. Susan, the divorcee, is in recovery. She wants to find some peace after a long period of emotional trauma. Tony is a corporate lawyer. He feels he is losing "his soul" in a gauntlet of business dealings. Monica, an energy healer, wants to find a way to be more effective in the world. Karla and Doreen are a lesbian couple trying to rekindle the spark between them that somehow seems lost. Dax is a cinematographer and "looking for adventure". Everyone has a tale.

We chat amongst ourselves over meals and before group sessions. On the third day, I receive a gift: I sit with Sedona. She asks me to tell her my story. In another world, she is a therapist and author. She is simply lovely. I trust her from the moment I see her. In her late fifties, she has the crisp features and high cheek bones of an Apache chieftain. Her skin is tanned and worn, but it is not leath-

ery, as there is a simple blush that comes from within that makes her seem younger. Her voluminous raven black hair has swaths of grey. It is braided and put up fashionably. Taken together she looks like an ageless woman warrior. The energetic I sense around her is at once fierce and tender. I feel safe as we sit face to face.

She asks me what has called me to the desert. I say, "I want to be of service and need direction." She smiles and says that such requests often come with a price tag attached. "Are you willing to do anything to honor Spirit?" she asks. Before I can answer, she adds, "I don't want you to tell me, just be aware that the gods are picky, but when you are called, they will make sure that you are tough enough to do the work. There is always a price for being picked."

The core of the trip is a solitary three-day silent fast. In the days before, we stake out our locations. We each haul gallon jugs full of precious water to our temporary home. My space is just to the south of the base camp, below a low cliff, in the shadow of a larger bluff. Nestled in a small canyon, I feel something in the land that speaks to me. I have no fluency with this type of thing, but it calls and I answer. I suspect that that exchange contains the essence of this whole journey. When I share this with Sedona, she nods, and says, "Learn to listen to the land, it will not lie." On my explorations, I find a freshly shed snake skin. I proudly show it to one of the assistants who is here just to help with the cooking and the rituals. Her eyes get big,

and she says, "Wow, that is something special. Looks like you are heading into a new life." In my naive way, I do not know what to make of it, or her response. Years later, I am only beginning to understand.

The fast and alone time begin with drumming, sage, and a farewell blessing. Each of us, in silence, heads out in the early light to our new home to find our destiny. It will not be an easy seventy-two hours for me. I will get sick to my stomach; it will rain, I will be tired, and pitiful. But, in the midst, I will find that if I strip naked and lie with my belly on the earth, I feel better. I will find that as the moon comes over the crest of the mountain, that it awakens me, and there is some deep reassurance from within while watching it rise. I will journal and find some pattern in what seems to be a random life. There will be some deep feeling that begins to form, that somehow, I am part of a larger pattern.

The last day, I will lug large rocks to a central space. I will create a circle. Each rock will represent a person, place, or thing that resonates in my life. I will have one for my family, my AA group, my dog, my house. Things that are active in my life will form this circle, and, as the sun sets, I will place the last rock, that represents me, and I will sit. I will stay awake through the night, literally "sitting in my life". I will doze, but remain conscious of what seems like a traffic of spirits and dreams that wash over me. Dawn will come suddenly, and it will be time to return. I will kiss the land before I leave. I will place a crystal that I have

brought with me into the ground to honor the space. For this will have been a spot that called to me. It will have supported me as I have done hard work. There will be the sense of the awakening of an energetic between me and Something Else. It will be the first time that I begin to understand that such things exist.

The tired band of questers struggles in. We each are truly happy to see the others. We embrace like lost family. We *are* lost family. We eat a wondrous meal of stew and bread. It is fresh, hot, and homemade. We then sit in a circle and tell our stories. We do this very formally, in third person. I am one of the first: "He came to the desert to find guidance." I say, and over what seems like hours, my story comes flooding out. I tell of my fears about being too small, about staying sober, about being a good husband and father. I tell of the struggles I have of thinking that I am being called to do something specific, but not knowing what that is. I explain how I have felt tended to during my time in the desert. That for the first time in my life, I have sensed a connection between me and Something massive. I tell of the joy of being woken up by the moon as it rises. Sedona then repeats what she has heard from me. She then gives me a blessing and reassurance. Finally, she says, "You have a given name, and then a name that defines your truth. By the grace of What brought you here, I name you: 'Dances Under the Moon'."

I feel at peace, and for once, at home in the world. The trip ends almost abruptly. We go back to our day to day,

and undergo what is called "re-entry". I email my new friends and Sedona. Each time I receive a reply, I feel a renewal and a sense of calm. Sedona has touched me in a deep way. What is more, she and the experience have shepherded me into an initiation. I am opened to a world of Spirit, and I could never have imagined it before.

Several years later, she is killed in a car wreck while doing mission work in Africa. Not long after that, she begins to come to me in my dreams. She remains with me now as a guide and counselor. Each time I need help or direction, she seems to find me.

When I remember the whole trip, I recall with a special happiness the last night. We all sit as a group in a large circle around a flaming bonfire. Sedona recounts what we have done, and then asks each of us by name to swear a sacred oath. Under that moon, in that remote desert place, I swear: "Whenever Spirit calls I will answer, regardless of the consequences." In that moment, something shifts. Now, twenty years later, and deep into a transition to become a woman, I know this is a calling from Spirit. I can do nothing more than what I promised then: I say "yes," and gird my loins. Sedona is so very proud.

The Arc of a Lifetime

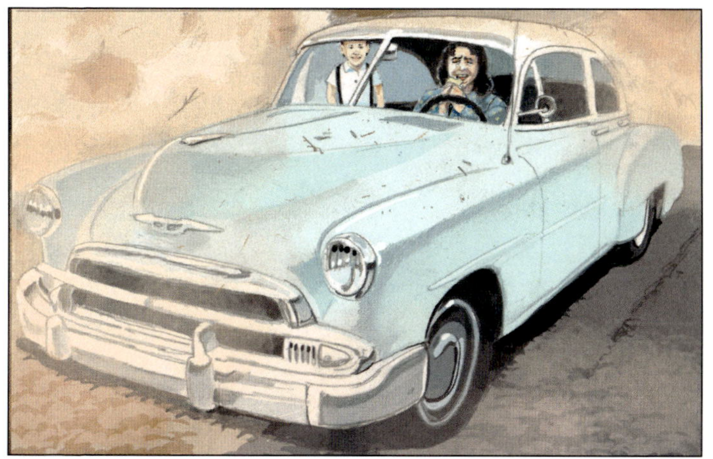

"The journey itself creates the message."

—PERSONAL JOURNAL, 10-16-1998

There are two memories that define the arc of my life. Both involve my mother. It was not until much later when grappling with my own issues, I understand that they involved her own struggle with a

calling. The first: it is 1954, and a late March afternoon in West Texas. It is near dark. My mother is in the driver's seat of a 1951 two-tone Chevrolet. The gear shift is in the column. I remember how shiny the knob is in the fading light. I am standing deathly still in the front seat; an arm's length separates us. I am in milk chocolate colored shorts with suspenders and a short-sleeved white tuck-in shirt. I have an off-white jockey cap that tilts back on my head, and scuffed, white leather shoes that rise just above my narrow ankles. Thin, clean, white socks are rolled back down to just over the top. My shoelaces are tied tight. My father has helped me with those earlier that morning. He cut my fingernails, too. I am studying the laces as the wind howls about us. We are in the midst of a screaming sandstorm. The dirt and grit, thick and powerful like a machine, sandblasts the car. It sounds like thousands of voices whispering as the dirt beads across the windshield. I cannot see past the hood, and it only adds to the feeling, the knowing: we are all alone.

My mother is sobbing. Her thin, white hands shake as she wales. Her fingernails, impeccably done in blood red. The sobs at times are louder than the wind; then they drown out with a crescendo. An ebb and flow of pain and chaos. I do not know why we are parked on the side of this small Texas highway on this dirt filled, late spring day. I reach over and gently touch her shoulder. The blue cotton dress is starched and the folds impeccable with sharp creases, like that of the nurse attire she wears in a

photo I later find in the attic. She shakes her head as I pat her heaving shoulder. I say, "It will be ok." She just rocks, shakes her head, and sobs.

Years later, I see this from the windshield looking in. All in clear relief. I see each detail and hear each moan. We are on the side of the road in a raging storm, and my mother is lost in her own pain. What is this all about? For a long time, I had no idea. But, at that point, I do know that she felt lost and afraid and, perhaps, as I touch her shoulder, it is as close as I will ever come to really seeing her while she was alive.

Flash forward sixty years. I walk into room 777 at the hospital. It is the day after Christmas 1992. I am still nearly drunk on Chivas and red wine, and thirty minutes late. In that half hour, my mother has wheezed and begun to breathe long, slow, and cumbersome breaths. They become less frequent. The seasoned nurse sees this, she stops, sits down, and holds my mother's hand. The head nurse comes in and stands by my father. His best friend and roommate of forty-two years is in the last minutes of a brief three-month pais de deux with small cell cancer of the lung. It has spread in this time. A metastasis to the brain came first, and a hideous one to the right femur appeared later. It is this latter one invading the bone that is problematic. The pain filled wailing that she has with the unseen demons is the same that I had heard that day in the sandstorm. The Cheyne-Stokes respirations, shallow and halting, have been on and off for a week. But, this is

different, and my father and those sweet nurses know that. When she passes, he cannot bear to leave her side. Several other nurses finally drag him next door. It is then that I arrive. As I walk in, the nurse tries to shield me, but realizes I am "the doctor".

Her dead body seems so alien. It is a drab, sullen, grey mannequin. There is no resemblance to the loving and animated entity that resonated in that form for many years. Death is here to lay claim.

As they undress her and bathe the dried blood from the old central line site, she looks so small, so vulnerable. This body has born me into this world. So foreign but somehow human. I never remember seeing her this clearly. It is as if I had always seen a projection, never the real thing. But, I am drunk and have missed my mother's last breath, and the first tears of my father's life in the world without his best friend.

Twenty-one years later, I sit bent over in a chair crying in deep, inconsolable sobs just after telling the one I love that I am a woman. Neither of us understands anything about what that means.

I Wonder

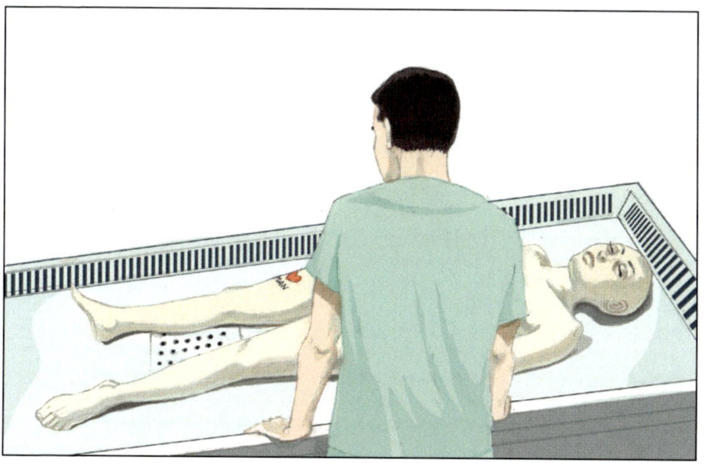

I am nothing, just a mirror in the palm of your hand,
reflecting your kindness, your sadness, your anger.
If you were a blade of grass or a tiny flower
I will pitch my tent in your shadow.
Only your presence revives my withered heart.
You are the candle that lights the whole world
and I am an empty vessel for your light.

—RUMI

The memory is a very clear one. I am four years old, I wake and both my parents are standing next to my bed. They are so young and fresh. Content and happy, we are all in our comfortable, two bedroom, brownish-red brick house on 17th Street. My father asks one question: "What would you like to do today?" I say, without hesitation, "I want to make something."

I am such an industrious child. My parents, such forward thinkers, make a grand work area in my small bedroom. It is a large, flat surface made from a three-foot by six-foot old pink door. For years I will carve, paint, glue, and dissect a myriad of projects, large and small, in that space. How wise they are. In this way, they validate one thing that is critical to my growth: curiosity. These are the years I look for quartz crystals in the red dirt, read Doctor Dolittle, learn piano, make candles, carve balsa wood figures, fashion models of the human body, learn photography, write stories, and do cross-stitching. I spend whole summer days exploring the canyon just a block away. I learn the trees, the type of birds, and insects. I find where the gourds grow, where rain pools, and the hiding places of the odd looking horned toads that are so plentiful. The residue of such unbridled curiosity is something resonant. My parents give me the freedom to create wonder.

Someplace in the years I spend in school, I lose that gift. I become enamored with definition. I learn rules, classifications, set theorems, and facts. Rote memoriza-

tion gives me confidence. I pass tests, make good grades, and receive recognition. The more I define things, the less ambiguity I encounter. In this way, the world is safer, less threatening. It becomes second nature to become reductionist in all encounters. In this process, I wander far away from the feminine intuitive and feeling functions that are so much a part of curiosity and wonder. I find great comfort in the masculine imperatives where I make judgment and assign value. My ego becomes active in marshaling a hierarchy of all things. Everyone and everything has its place in this world of mine.

It is sad that my medical training supports such thinking. In pathology and physiology, we break things down to basic levels. We learn cell types, organs, organ systems, then systemic processes. Each is seen as something apart. As well, for every action there is a specific reaction that can be predicted, if knowledge of the initial conditions is known. Cause always equals effect and pathology is organ specific. The first casualty in my training: my ability to find wonder in the human condition.

It is August 1979. Three of my medical school classmates and I stand over a dead woman. We share a cadaver that is kept in a silver, stainless steel tank. The body rests on a seven-foot slab which can be lowered or raised. This way it can be examined, dissected, or pushed down into the recess of the tank. We literally whittle on this body for a year. By the end, there are only bits and pieces of greasy body parts floating in formaldehyde in the dark tank.

In the act of dissection, more seems lost than just the body parts. Granted, I have learned each nerve and the position and angle of all bones, tendons, and muscles, but at what cost? The integrity, something related to the whole, is lost in the venture.

It is many years later that I remember that our cadaver has a distinguishing tattoo on her thigh. It is a two-inch heart on the right upper leg. Just under it is inscribed one word: "MAN". The questions that I have now seem so different from those I had then. I wonder what brought her to such a thing? Tattoos were not common in those days, especially for women. Was this the name of a lover or friend? Perhaps a declaration of a devotion to humanity as a whole. Was it a lusting for anything masculine? Did she give aforethought and make ritual the marking of her body? Or, was she drunk out of her mind and did it on a whim one dull night? I don't know the answers to any of these things, but I do know that I am so sad that I gave that tattoo only passing interest. I used that body. I attacked the sural nerve and its path, and the muscles of the eye, and the placement of the pancreas just behind the stomach. Yet I never bothered to honor the sanctity of this human nor the sacredness of her journey to that final resting place just under my scalpel. I wonder about it now.

Why do I think of all this? Perhaps I am made more sensitive by my own odd journey to be a woman. I know that for so many years I was arrogant toward and dismissive of so many people and things that were lower in my

pyramid of life's hierarchy. I gave no thought to how my ego leaps and lusts to operate in this way. Master of my own universe, I assign value to all things. I find relief in the certainty that it creates for me. It is a narrow world, but comfort is the first imperative. I lose my curiosity in small doses.

My gender transition experience and its relationship with my family is something that has a life of its own. It, like the body in my anatomy class, has distinguishing features and angles that make it more memorable. It has a history that accommodates multiple and often competing narratives; but, it is always something recognizable, even at a distance. Especially at a distance. At times, certain parts have been examined in detail. But, at some point, the core of the relationship is dissected, teased, and resected to a point that it is simply not coherent. Is it a male? A female? Was this father or mother? Who knows?

We each have a desperate need for something that comes from interpreting a part in the whole. But the paradox is that none of us has the same feeling about the experience. The whole, like the woman under the scalpel, has a sanctity that must be honored that cannot be discerned from individuated ego-driven needs. Consumed in a mind driven frenzy of discovery, in the end, there is little left of what it once was. It will have to be buried. It may or may not be resurrected. But, the truth: it was a vessel to carry love. The experience of that love is most important, but it is only reflected as an aspect of the whole.

It is February 1996. My father answers the telephone in a condominium that he leases in San Diego. "Are you related to John Oliver?" an older female voice asks in a shy tone. He says, "John Oliver was my father, we all called him Jack. Why do you ask?"

"My name is Mary, I was engaged to him, and I loved him more than anything. That has been many, many years ago, but I still live with his image. I just wanted to talk to someone who knew him to see how things turned out in his life." My father, the good man that he was, meets readily with Mary.

My grandfather, one of the first flight instructors in the Army Air Corps, is stationed in San Diego. He is there for two years. I can picture him now in his bi-plane. He flies low over the crest of Sunset Cliffs, dives down to nearly touch Mission Beach, gains altitude and follows the coast up to Del Mar. In the warm spring air, he sees the dolphins jumping in La Jolla Cove and the majestic strawberry fields covering the mountains just inland. At Encinitas, he turns back south. Further out, he watches the sun rise over the eastern horizon. Twenty-two years old and master of his own destiny, he knows who and what he is: a young man and a pilot. He flies like he lives: fully present and with abandon. He is in love with his life, and with a pretty, auburn-haired woman named Mary. They are to be married at some future point. Thinking, like the young often do, only of the day ahead, he banks on the soft, west wind and lands gently.

Mary, according to my father, waits for Jack to return from Texas after he leaves the service. He never comes back. Heart broken, she becomes a teacher, marries, raises two good men, and lives a solid life. She retires with her husband, who is a kind-hearted mate. They share years of domestic travel until he dies suddenly. She is left alone.

Remarkably, through all the years, she has never given up the love that she holds for John Oliver. She closets it like a sacred mandala, and brings it out to examine only in the confines of her heart, when she is alone, or needs comfort. In her narrative, he is the deep, masculine, hero who anchors a good portion of her life. She carries this projection like a talisman buried deep within her consciousness. She is guilty only of tenacity and need for love.

Images, like experiences, relationships, and, bodies, are malleable. They can be embellished or defaced in a myriad of ways, thus losing the truth that they once held. Mary holds a conscious picture of my grandfather, taken at twenty-two, for over sixty years! That image never ages and is never tainted. She builds a story around it and constructs an entire parallel universe. It is one in which her prince charming will one day return. Young and healthy, they will elope and live, happily ever after, on love.

We are all capable of such vital constructs. Each of us carries the images of people, places, and things that remain vivid, yet are concretized in a moment in time. For instance, there are places in the world where mummified bodies of family live in the home and are treated as if alive.

They are honored, and periodically even their clothes are changed. If the embalming is adequate, the body can remain static in decay and change little over decades.

It seems we humans are so much in need of something solid and lasting. Is it any wonder that we project onto images and experiences which gratify us a timelessness? Even if unreliable, the need seems reflexive. We can also deconstruct experiences and people in the same way. Conflict, ambiguity, and time are constants that tend to diminish our memories of the acts and people we once held in high regard.

I am cleaning out the storage place that holds thousands of photos from my past. Such images, like the tattoo on my cadaver, like my family experiences, can carry my projections. But, because of the rigid way in which they are forced into the psyche, they tend to rebel. They disappoint. Those still living that I put on a pedestal must be given room to grow and change. If not, there comes a point where the capacity to hold those projections is overwhelmed. My images are such fragile things. They keep me warm in the dark days of my journey but bind me with a false sense of comfort that they were never meant to convey.

From the depths of the steel tank of that anatomy lab, a voice whispers back to me: "Do not become trapped in the images and pieces of your life. If you do, wonder and curiosity will evade you. What you seek will be lost. For it is only in considering the *whole* that your soul may be found."

First Blush

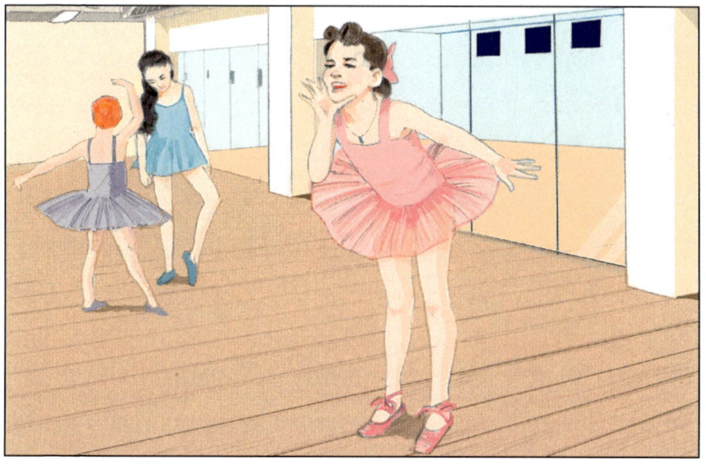

"*At the center of your being you have the answer; you know who you are and you know what you want.*"

—LAO TZU

It is the end of April 1956. The day is wild with wind. Sand fills the Martian looking sky. I am at a private school for dance and nearing the end of the first grade. We all are grouped in a small, red-shingled house. It squats on two lots facing east. There is no grass, only gravel. A

giant jungle gym looms in the south-side yard just next to a fading white, painted swing set. From inside, I hear the noisy squeaking of the chains as the swings blow high in the air with the raging wind. The front part of the house, the size of two large bedrooms, is a well-buffed hardwood and varnished floor. It is an open studio with balance beams stalking the perimeter. Mirrors hang floor to ceiling. Everything is reflected.

There I learn tap, a little ballet, and some modern dance steps. But most of all I feel like one of the girls. I crave the camaraderie as much as the popsicles. I see nothing wrong with fitting in with Jill, Jenna, Ann, and Melissa. Women I will come to know for a lifetime. For me, these two early years are deeply special. I jump out of bed each morning and run from the blue Mercury station wagon looking forward to being one among. I dance, I sing, I laugh, I color, I read, I write. All among a sweet cluster of kindred spirits. These are years I feel most at home in the world.

My teacher is just over forty, I suspect. She has big, green eyes, a grand, electric smile, plump red lips, and black-framed oval glasses that somehow make her look angelic. Her mother, a formal and rigid woman, is over seventy. With fitted false teeth, dull-gray hair lumped under a flat dark bonnet, and a pugnacious chin, she is our mother superior. No one crosses her. No one.

The end of the year is so very special. In February, notices go out to parents with instructions about the "End of Year Dance Recital." It is specific guidance about

material to be bought, places of fitting, times of try-ons, practices, and dress rehearsals. It is a grand event. My mother drives to Woolworth's downtown, just near the bank, to get swaths of blue, yellow, cream, and chocolate colored silk before they run out. For two months, a saint of a seamstress patiently sizes, sews, and resizes the costumes for a score of stars to be.

I can see the outfits now. One has light blue shorts and a bright yellow shirt for "I Am My Daddy's Pride and Joy". The other has silky smooth, dark-chocolate shorts and top, and a cream-colored hat for "Little Chocolate Soldier". They are so very soft and the silk feels so sumptuous.

There are six of us standing in a straight line on the large stage. The bright lights shield the full auditorium from us; but, I feel the energy. I tap, kick, tap, turn, kick, and bow. I sing in a high off-key voice, "And I am, my Daddy's first and most, I am my Daddy's pride and joy! Wheeee." Turn, kick, stand, bow.

Most of all I see the hours just before the performances. With dress rehearsal and real performance alike, the teacher puts on our make-up. Ever so carefully, ever so slowly. Rumor has it that she has been in Hollywood in some capacity. One thing is certain: she knows her stuff. She has a special pedestal built just for us! I walk up three steps, and "stand tall" so that she does not have to bend over to apply the foundation, blush, and lipstick.

I mount those steps as if called to heaven. The first year, I don't know what to expect. By the second, I count

the days till I go to receive that most special blessing: my make-up. Both years, though, after loving application of a soft, liquid foundation, she takes a large, soft brush and liberally applies powder. Under my eyes, around the nose, then on my throat. She stands back, smiles then fills in the spots that need tending. Next comes a hot pink blush that she taps on with a flourish. Finally, the golden tube: a bright, slick, ruby red lipstick. It is almost too much to bear. I then stand in front of the large mirrors lining the studio and stare at the lovely being I have become. At some deep level, I knew that it was *me*. It will take many years to remember how it felt to have on that make-up.

The final year, the ending of the recital is traumatic. I know there will be no further opportunity to mount the steps. Sadly, there is no way to repeat that magic. I try to hide, then make excuses that I am looking for something that I have lost, just so I don't have to take off the make-up. I am young, but I find something that is me, truly me, and now, I must give it up. I am so full of mixed emotions. I am so happy and content with being me; but, I am torn about what this all means.

Ambivalence at six years of age is what stays with me. Tragically, there was simply no way for me to communicate the depth and complexity of the feelings that were exploding within. The residue was a longing that never quite went away. But at some level, I knew from that point forward what it felt like to be happy and content. For me, it has always included lipstick and blush.

"Fifty cents short of a chicken leg."

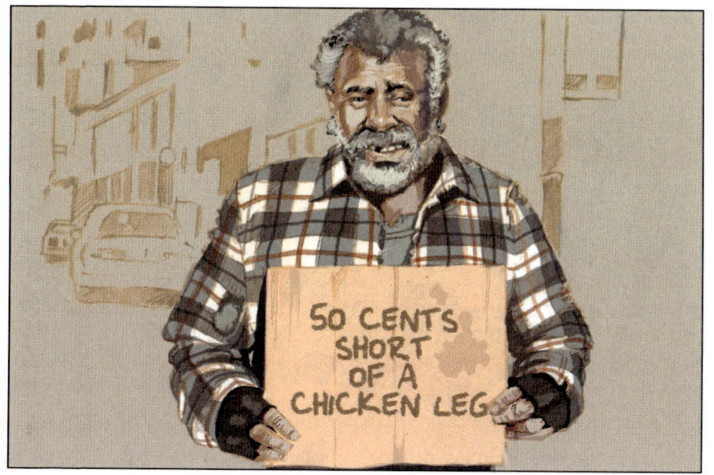

"You can't go home again."

—THOMAS WOLFE

When I was young, David was my best friend. We were inseparable. We ate and slept at the other's house. We told each other secrets. The friendship was my ballast. With the ebb and flow of

hormones, growing bodies in flux, random deaths of pets and grandparents, it was a sacred constant. He lived on 14th Street at the end of a cul-de-sac that sloped up from Douglas Street. Bill lived to the west and Russ across the street. How odd both of them are dead now. Such a thing would have been impossible to consider at that age: friends live forever.

David's house sits on the high ground. On clear days with no adults around, we scamper up the wooden fence to the top of the flat roof. You can see the entire world from here. The small mountain to the west, the big hospital to the north, that giant water tower at the Veterans Administration to the south. Best of all: you can look straight down into the canyon just below. It spreads out like another universe. It is a gift to have some space to call home. It is not a territorial modifier, it is an anchor to some deeper longing. Whatever the weather or time of year, standing on top of that perch I belong to a *place*.

Home-land is more than a descriptive; it is a part of our DNA. There is an emotional and spiritual overlay that does not dissipate. I still have flashbacks about looking for quartz crystals in that canyon, making lead medallions by melting old Christmas tree icicles in a hidden fire, and carving ornamental cups by hollowing out the large squash gourds found in late spring and early summer in the shadows of the ravines.

That house was the departure point for my first adventure. Late one spring morning, a new house keeper for

David's family announces to me that it is "time to go home." Before I can protest, she pushes me out the door. There I stand. I am three whole blocks from home. In my mind, it is an impossibly difficult journey. How can I ever find my way? It will take a lifetime. There is the issue of a street crossing, the two massive dogs, and, the unknown. These are unimaginable obstacles. I am afraid.

I stand on the slope of the hill and look down to the bottom. At that point I am halfway across the River Styx; neither dead nor alive, I cannot tread water for infinity. A choice must be made. I shake my head, and there is an anticipation of the long journey before me. Yet, there is also a comfort I feel. This feels right. Trust and go. Trust and go. Something deep encourages me, and I respond. It is as if I know I am already finished.

I toddle down the hill, step into the street, and begin. It takes maybe twenty minutes, but, by the time I reach my house, I am forever changed. Proud of what I have done, I know now what a calling feels like. What is more, I know the joy in honoring that call. At that age, I cannot share it with another soul, as I suspect trouble will follow. But, that is a life lesson, too: the hard things one does alone. The residue is a confidence that is not forgotten. It is the base element I will use countless times on the road ahead. The construct will not change: I just want to get home. The paths will vary, but the need remains the same.

It is a summer day in the 1980's. I am in New Mexico, deep in the pine-covered mountains south of Albuquerque.

My parents own a house there. From the balcony, you can see the beautiful apricot and teal blue sunsets and smell the ozone from the river below. That time of the year there is always the threat of a summer rain. It can be torrential. A brief, but massive downpour can fill up the fickle stream. In the blink of an eye, the murmuring brook turns into a white-water rapid.

Late on this day, a rainstorm drops several inches in less than an hour. The low-water crossing that bears most traffic will be closed, I think, as I drive toward town to get groceries. The local police surely have blocked off the feeder road that leads to deeper water. They always do. But the police are not timely on this day. However, there is a Good Samaritan stopping traffic to warn others about the high water just around the bend. He has an old, wizened face that is kind. I imagine he has done such good deeds most all of his life. I roll down the window to hear his warning just as an old pick-up zooms around us. Thirty feet beyond, the driver slams on the brakes and backs up with speed. The window rolls down. It is an older, Caucasian male, disheveled, irritated, red-faced. He shouts, "How high's the water?" The Good Samaritan says, "Too high to cross." The old man pauses, shakes his head, and says, "I don't care, my wife is sick. I have to get home." He heads off. The next day they find his body nearly a mile downstream.

I wonder what it felt like to pull out into that raging stream in that old pick-up. To have it stall, the cold water

beginning to gush into the cab. The panic, the hyperventilation, the fear, the last-ditch effort to restart the engine, the rolling down of the window, the desperation as the current drags him away without any chance to take a breath. I wonder in the chaos of those final minutes if he thought of his wife? Just trying to get home.

Recently, I stopped at a light here in my hometown. There are few intersections these days that do not have one or more people holding signs and asking for money. Only occasionally do I feel guilt that I have grown insensitive to the heartache that stands three feet from me at each one of those points. But, this day, I look over and there is an older black man. He has a gray beard and wears a dirty fatigue jacket. He is slumped, shoulders are hunched and he looks to be dead tired. I see it in the way he stands and in the stare he has. He is beat-up and on his last reserve. I read this pitiful sign: "Homeless, and fifty cents short of a chicken leg." I roll down the window and give him a five-dollar bill and say something generic. But, that man haunts me still. He was lost, and hungry for home, and home cooking. He was in Purgatory.

These days I have transgender transition problems, money seems to be an irritant, I struggle not to lose my temper when driving, I worry about my family. These are living problems that come with the journey I guess. But, somewhere I still have a dream and goals. I just know I can make it from David's house to 17th Street. Sure, I know I will get washed away someday, but in the meantime, I

don't want to arrive at that point where I lose that great treasure called hope.

If I have learned any truth from this long journey, it is this: in these desperate days, I must be kind to myself and to others, because fifty cents short of a chicken leg is a descriptive for so many lives; and, the reality is that we are all here together, each just trying to get home.

The Catcher

"A mentor is someone who allows you to see the hope inside yourself."

—OPRAH WINFREY

It is a weekday afternoon in April 1958. In the small West Texas town wind howls and dust kicks high in the warm spring sky. My Dad, his Lucky Strike nestled gently between the fingers of his right hand, easily shifts the gears on the column in the old red and white Ford Bronco. "Where are we going now, Daddo?" I ask. He says, "You'll see." He smiles that soft smile. We stop in front of a sand colored, stucco house, on the east side of Goliad Street. From there you can see a sloping mountain guarding everything from the west. To the north, the big hotel towers over all of downtown. It houses the local brothel, but it will be a handful of years before I know what that mystery means.

This is an innocent time. I love my Dad. Most every afternoon, I ride my bike the two blocks from our house

on 17th Street to see him. Our grocery store is located on the main business artery of town. It is the epicenter of our family universe. We "go for coffee" at the pharmacy across the street where he listens to the highlights of my day as I drink sweet lemonade made fresh behind the long counter.

Years later, I will remember this day as I think about something that T.S. Eliot said, "Every moment is a fresh beginning." Looking back it captures the essence of the day. Daddo has taken off early. To do that in the afternoon with hours of work still ahead is not an ordinary thing. I do not know, but I am being driven to meet the first alpha-male, not related, that will influence my life. My beloved Pop, my Dad's father, was my first mentor. But, he is five months away from an early smoker's death. I will need other guides.

Benson opens the screen door before we can knock. He is my new little league coach. I don't know what Benson's first name is, or if that *is* his first name. I call him "Sir," but every adult just calls him "Benson". He is square and has a power that is unanticipated. Not more than 5'8", his belly is tight over a broad cowboy buckle. He has steel blue eyes and hands thick with callouses. He works at the refinery. It is backbreaking, thankless, grunt work; always six days a week. Several teeth are missing. He smokes Winston cigarettes with a long, long drag and slow exhale. He seems to think as he smokes, and he smokes constantly. As time goes on, like so many men

in that small town, he seems so solid in a natural way. His spirit announces to the world: "I am who I am." You know with a single look that he is a man among men. It seems people like that are a true force of nature. With a macho energetic, he lives uncontested.

At this time of life, I am deep under the protective wing of feminine forces. My mother and maternal grandmother, with whom I spend a good deal of time, marshal them in a fluid, if in-obvious way. I take piano lessons, cross-stitch, learn photography, and make candles and jewelry. I miss the camaraderie of my female friends at the private school of dance. Benson, the alpha-male, mirrors a balancing force. He is the archetypal masculine. Unbeknownst to him or to me, he balances my psyche at a critical point in time. If the feminine goes unopposed much further, I likely drift away from any chance of ever hearing the warrior call that will so define the arc of my life. Yin meets yang that day.

He "shushes" his dog and flashes us a big grin. He has been at the tryout of eight-year-old aspiring baseball players the previous Saturday. The six coaches draw lots to determine picking order, then they each choose until everyone is on a team. He picks me first.

There must have been several scores of kids there that dusty morning taking grounders off a fungo bat on a hard dirt infield infested with rocks the size of walnuts. Perched on the safe side of the backstop, he watches with the other coaches to see who can follow the ball and adjust

on the move. He sees me pick up the twenty-eight-inch pinewood "Al Kaline" bat with the green knob then line shots into left field. Whack after whack. I have a gift. He sees it. Benson needs a catcher first and foremost. Later he will say it only took him a second to figure it out. I have just what it takes.

We walk into his small living room. Laid out on the lime-green linoleum floor are a mask, two shin guards, and a chest protector. He even has a protective plastic cup with a small jockstrap laid to the side. My Dad smiles at Benson, squints a little and nods what seems to be approval at something not said. Benson asks him something about business, and then he turns his attention to me and shakes my hand. It is solid and he means it man-to-to man. It has that weighty firmness of authority. I am honored.

He just looks at the gear and then at me. He laughs a deep two-pack-a-day laugh and says in his deep, frog like voice: "You need to be a catcher, you hear?" It is really not a question. It is simple and direct. Like the voice of God: "Here you go, this is what you are, now learn to be with it."

They call the catcher's paraphernalia the "tools of ignorance". It is named that for a good reason. Donning the seven pounds of protection to have someone throw a hard sphere at you is not easy to learn. Done for hours at a time in the dry heat of a West Texas summer afternoon with a bat inches away from one's head demands special and severe discipline, or ignorance.

It never made any difference to me. Benson gave me

the keys to a kingdom. He knew and, I suspected, that the catcher controls the whole rhythm and flow of a magical realm. From that day as a bright-eyed eight-year-old, till the last game I played as the captain of my college team, I loved every single second of every single game and practice. In those sixteen years, I throw and receive tens of thousands of balls. I catch soft throwing left handers, right handers with blazing speed, and even some defiant knuckleballers. I play in a good high school league, then semi-pro ball in the summer in Dallas, against grizzly veterans who have washed out of Double A ball and college kids trying to learn to hit a curve. I go to a camp in Irving for a month most years. There, one bright morning I catch a soft toss from the iconic Bob Feller. Later, I play against Ivy Leaguers who will go on to play pro ball, and others that will go on to run companies with more income than small nations.

I play a scrimmage game against the Mets in the spring of 1970. It is the year after they have won it all and will, over time, become legends: "The Miracle Mets". A young kid still trying to make the club throws a ball one hundred miles per hour and it hits me on my wrist. I have never seen anything remotely like that fastball. Years later I can tell others that I got on base against Nolan Ryan. That at-bat was a very important bifurcation point for me. For years, I had cultivated a hidden fantasy that I could play baseball professionally. Seeing those two pitched balls delivered with that velocity, my dreams are decimated. I am forever

certain that I could never have made a living playing the game I love so much. Despite the years of devotion and dedication, there are physical gifts that others have that I do not. Nothing can compensate. In that one brief at-bat, baseball teaches me a truth that applies to all endeavors: there is a hierarchy of abilities.

But, looking back to those thousands of innings, those hundreds of thousands of balls caught and thrown, I love the feeling of looking out from my squatted position to guide the action. I tell the pitcher what to throw, I set up my mitt to target where it should go. I holler at the batter to swing at all manner of pitches. I direct the infield and outfield alike to shift or play straight away. I study the batters, how they approach the plate, where they position their feet, the arc of their swing, and whether or not they "dig in". I can keep them loose and hesitant with balls just inside or back them completely away if need be. I can leave them crying at the umpire when a soft curve drops just on the black part of the plate and a "Strike three!" echoes from "blue".

Years later, in a March 1994 journal entry, I write this about baseball: "I was drawn to the old park. And there I stood on a barren, cold infield. Dark clouds were about, and freezing mist was bearing down. I realized then that this diamond, this plot of land, somehow missed my love. There was an essence, and it demanded more than the heroics I created on summer nights. It wanted reciprocity. I woke up to the linkage between me and Something much

larger. It was, and is, a window to a larger universe and a mirror reflecting back to me my own desires and behaviors. It demanded a payment for this insight: a just and honest love. Only in retrospect do I understand the sacredness of the relationship. I was a guardian of this sacred sport. I loved it, and I loved how it made me feel a part of Something much larger. This was a masculine realm. Foreign as it was to the interior fluency that I felt with the feminine forces within, it was a process with symmetry and flow and consequence. The cold winter days I drive out to the ballpark and lay on my back on home plate and stare into the grey and looming clouds, I am given some sense that this Force misses me. It needs some reassurance that it is not forgotten. It needs affirmation that there are warmer days ahead where I can live into the potential that is the construct of this matrix we call life. It is only in that way that the Sacred becomes manifest. Until then it has only the possibility of creating grace."

In reality, it was my first taste of a calling. These many years later, I remain grateful for Benson. He was a guide into that realm and channeled some Spirit that caught hold of us both. It is a resonance that has shifted and morphed into other forms. It never has, and never will, leave my heart.

"Folks like me."

In every man, there is something which to a certain degree
prevents him from becoming perfectly transparent to himself;
and this may be the case in so high a degree,
he may be so inexplicably woven into relationships of life
which extend far beyond himself that he almost cannot
reveal himself.
But he who cannot reveal himself cannot love,
and he who cannot love is the most unhappy man of all.

—SOREN KIERKEGAARD

It is June 1960. My beloved Grandma is driving us to our mountain home in the cool pines of New Mexico. It is the first week of summer. The numinous blue sky crowds out all other forms. The vistas of the Sangre de Cristo Mountains are not yet clear; it will be another forty miles of scrub and flat land before they blossom in the west like giant purple mushrooms. I am a pre-teenager with a life and dreams untethered. Three months of joy lie ahead. I will fish for trout in the bubbling stream behind

the split-log cabin, play miniature golf till blisters form, eat pancakes with abandon, and watch cartoons late into the morning. I am young and invincible.

We stop to eat at a diner in Tatum, New Mexico. Along for the trip is Annie Ruth, my surrogate mother. Because I have working parents, she comes to our house most days to cook and clean. She is honest and open, and I love her like family. She *is* family. As we eat our chicken fried steaks, I realize that Annie is not seated. I ask my wise grandmother about her. She says in a quiet voice, "She has to eat in the back." I am puzzled, but don't think anything more about it until I go to the bathroom. On the way back, I see Annie sitting at a dirty cardboard table in the kitchen. How odd. Eating a hamburger, she is talking with another woman who is busy washing dishes. I say, "Why don't you come sit with us?" She looks down and says in a hurt voice, "Folks like me have to stay back here."

For the first time in my short life, I am shown and see: either/or. She is black, I am white. Suddenly, there is a difference. The innocence of ubiquity sees only unlimited potential. Until that moment all things are possible. Never again. There are limits and boundaries that have consequence. I never saw it before, but now could not forget.

Years later while living in Italy I will experience an earthquake. In an instant the land and air jar and tilt. Everything is shifted. That day in a greasy spoon of a cafe in the flatlands, there was an interior force of similar magnitude. It did not change the way I loved and

honored Annie, yet it shifted the way that I experienced her. It will fester for years; an infinity of subtle, culturally shaped judgments about race, sex, gender, and religion will compete in my mind. I had seen the way things work. The ego-driven modifiers always demand a hierarchy. All things are not equal.

It is a Thursday afternoon in 1989. I am off doctoring duty for a long weekend. I have come to a local strip club. Watching a young female, there is an ache, a longing that is more primal than sex. I have wrestled with this *something* on occasion. Never like this. Like oil bursting to the surface from the deep darkness of ancient sediment, a knowing erupts: "I don't want to have sex with her, I want to *be* her. I want to be a woman!" The alcohol has loosened long anchored bonds and critical boundaries. In the shadowy subterranean vaults of my psyche, I have felt this drumming, pounding essence since I was a child. But, never had it been so clear. For the briefest instant I want, more than anything, to be a woman. I quickly stuff that conscious revelation back deep within. I drink as if my life depends on it. Damping out the aftershocks that given expression will alter a life, I squash it with maniacal fervor. I will nearly die trying to suffocate it.

It is 2006. I sit with a thirty-something-year-old construction business owner and his wife. I explain what has prompted this urgent request for a meeting. The blood test results from labs done the day before have come back. He had been referred by a physician friend and

encouraged by his loving spouse who came with him. His chief complaint was vague: fatigue. There was pallor, but nothing concrete on exam. The lab calls me early the next morning. There is a critical value. The young man has severe kidney damage.

Think of it. He leaves for work a happy man. He has a loving wife and solid, young children. He is in no great debt. The big high school football game is this coming weekend. He will barbecue some ribs, drink some beer, get laid. He has years of good meals, a trusting family, and a prime hunting lease with his best friend to look forward to. He is Caucasian, a Methodist, strong, virile, and God-fearing. He is an alpha-male who is living the dream.

I do what I can to buffer the unfolding tragedy; but, then I say, "You need urgent dialysis." I will never forget the wailing cry of his wife, nor his twisted, sobbing face buried in those thick hands. In the blink of an eye, all the things he thought true about himself are swept away. All measures of his being are forever shifted. A subtle, genetic fault-line has slowly, methodically, twisted and morphed undetected until the kidneys fail. In an instant, his world explodes. There was safety and certainly in his mind that morning, an alternate reality has erupted by noon. By six in the evening he is bedded in the Intensive Care Unit watching his blood filter through a machine. Life as he knows it is forever swept away.

Fast forward to 2013. I have been sober and in therapy for over twenty years. I have the blessing of insight and

the gift of professional guidance. But, I am completely unprepared for the reemergence of the gender issue. For years it rumbles in the basement of my psyche. But, in time, I begin to sense something amiss. Am I crazy? Do I have a tumor? Is it a late-midlife crisis? I ignore it, like the flu or an unwanted rash. But I cannot forget the revelation in the strip club: "I want to be a woman." I continue to shove it deep into my psyche. Declaring I am a woman at this late point in life is unthinkable. But a day comes when not being true to myself is potentially fatal.

I become dysphoric and suicidal. Despite every measure of alpha-maleness that has shaped who I think I am, I must admit in the deepest way: I am a female. I make a choice, not around gender, but to save my life. I begin by owning what I am. To disarm the naysayers, I take batteries of tests, continue counseling and see a psychiatrist. Through it all: no new pathology is found and my cognition is intact.

The instant that this truth emerges, and once I own it, like my patient with kidney failure, my life is transformed. There are consequences: I am now a radical. If there is a rift within my conservative family, and with many cultured friends, then there are similar resonances in millions of other family units that suffer this same process. I see them reflected in the lives of transgender people whom I see as a volunteer physician in a clinic each week. Gender, even more than race, creed, health, or wealth, squats at the center of how we define others, and ourselves. It is

seemingly the heaviest single and most important factor in one's life; and, determines the arc of a lifetime. Today, it is a matrix that constellates the core of life experience.

But, what is it? People often get confused between the terms sex and gender. Sex refers to biological differences between males and females such as chromosomes (female XX, male XY), reproductive organs, and hormonal levels. Gender refers to the cultural differences expected by society of men and women according to their sex. A person's sex does not typically change from birth, but gender certainly can. Science has proven that many gender differences are learned and the assignment at birth carries a great deal of weight and influences on one's expectations, outlook, ethics, manners, vocabulary, and clothing. It shapes so much of what we can become. It can be changed, but there is massive inertia against this, and I feel that from the start.

I know now that my evolution represents to many a process antithetical to what is "right" and "just". It is a culturally polarizing issue. It surfaces in a period when so many of us cling rigidly to a world view in which this binary is absolute. As such, it is used politically to galvanize countless other issues. This is a dynamic we have grappled with for decades as it has the same underpinnings that civil rights activists found in trying to sit at the front of a bus or to enter a segregated school. It is the same monolithic force that my gay friends battled with church doctrines, military policy, and even states' rights.

Fortunately, we have begun to accommodate the fact that some people want to be intimate with others of the same sex; and, regardless of the color of skin, we all have equal rights. Don't we? Sadly, however much we think we have evolved, gender, like sexual preference and race, is a hidden tripwire that still detonates fatal explosions in families and institutions.

Having made a choice to pursue this to the end, I feel a deep certainty as I wade deeper into the world. For the first time in many years, I have a deep trust in my own moral compass. I had lost it, or worse, learned to ignore it. But, I had it when I saw Annie in the kitchen in that cafe in Tatum. I knew immediately: "This is not right."

It's time to step forward. I will not sit at the back of a dingy dive in the middle of nowhere and be treated differently because I am transgender. How odd, I am awake, and, God-forbid, I have become: "folks like me."

In My Face

"I understood why later, but, alas, too late."

—ZORBA THE GREEK

I am walking the path around Lady Bird Lake in downtown Austin. It is rowing season, and there are lanes laid out across the water for the competitive skulls that will race later in the day. As I walk, my perspective shifts. The white foot-long bobs that anchor the ropes begin to look like random debris filling the lake. Scores of white dots in a chaotic mess. But, as I move further, I can see from a different point, how the float lanes line up so elegantly. They define a perfect boundary.

For some reason, as I am thinking about this, I remember the times that I have been close to my own death. From a long way back these seem so random. But, from a certain perspective, further down the trail, they line up perfectly. Maybe near-death, like a calling, is just one of the markers in the fabric of my journey. Like the floats that I am looking at, they are built, by whatever Forces, to

create boundaries. All our days we fuss about negotiating these lanes that seem so radical and random. What am I here to do? Truth be known: I know so very little about what the true purpose of my life really is. It is as if I am pregnant and carry a sacred child with the capacity to transform the universe. But, I am only aware that I am nauseous a lot. I know this: only in retrospect do I see how the lanes lineup so precisely, side by side.

It is February 1969 in San Antonio. I am taking a test to get into West Point at Brooke Army Medical Center. With me are two other candidates. I drive the beige 1967 Skylark, a high school graduation gift from my parents. Music is turned up. We can get KOMA from Oklahoma City, "where the hits keep coming". We are in a newer residential part of town. Rural is hard to tell from urban, and there are streets that run headlong into the woods of the Texas Hill Country. I look to my left, and down a small, dark side street I see a lone figure running. It is near dusk, and there is just enough light to see detail. It is a Caucasian woman with long auburn hair. She is wearing nothing. Running naked.

"Holy shit," I scream, and turn to the left. We slow down and catch up with her. I keep her in the headlights as we drive down a paved street lined with bushes. As we crest a small hill she dodges and zags like a small animal, but does not stop nor turnaround. We keep her in the lights. With my friends screaming and whooping, we all hope she turns to show her tits. Finally, she looks over her shoulder.

Caught in the headlights, I will forever remember the look of terror. It reminds me of hunting rabbits on the golf course in a West Texas town on a hot summer night. A can of malt liquor in one hand, I turn on a spotlight and target the poor creature now running for its life. .22 caliber shots rain down. Lucky animals find a hole to dive into, but some, especially the old, pay for being slow and in the wrong place. There is such a random violence that runs in me, and in the world, and I can see neither at this point.

Years later, while in Africa I write in my journal: "I think animals sense how crazy we are and are terrified of the violence that we bear. They have a vital understanding of the schizophrenia, the drama, and the spectacle of random viciousness that we are addicted to. Sex and violence are what drive and direct us at an unconscious level. These creatures sense and understand in much clearer terms than we do ourselves." Sex and violence.

In the blink of an eye, he is at my window. "Stop, you mother fucker." I slam on the breaks. He is not a large man, but he has a fury about him that makes it feel like there is more than one. His short blond hair is wet, and he is so close that I smell his breath. It is heavy with liquor and cigarettes. He is unshaven. He has bad, crooked teeth, with a broad nose and tight lips. I suspect both have been busted many times before. He snarls, and heaves and there is the crackle of violence in the air. The .45 is an inch from my left temple. He shouts, "I'm killing all of you mother fuckers. That's my wife! You hear me?"

Strangely I am not afraid. Things slow down. I can see the muzzle and the dull sheen of the weapon. It will be years before I will learn the forensics, and come to know that the .45 slug splatters most all in its path for a good twenty meters. My brain will be spewed onto the inside of the car like a full pink, liquid filled, piñata. I see the black and gold tassel from my graduation cap dangling from the mirror and wonder if they will put that in my casket. I think, "I am going to die," but it does not register. I am too young and dumb and invincible and walled off at this stage of my life. I squirm and flatly say, "Sir, we were just trying to see if she needed help. We didn't know." It is not far from the truth. My two friends, one riding shotgun and the other in the back on the right side, stay hunkered down. There is pleading from the back seat: "Please don't shoot. Please don't shoot."

The woman has not stopped running. We have given her a head start on some deadly ramble. Unless this is a game the two play from time to time. I think of that. But, things slow further. The gun is still at my head; the music is still playing. I hear B.J. Thomas crooning "Hooked On A Feeling." I hear the heaving breath of the angry, violent, white man who has my life in his right hand. Who knows what has brought him here. Or what has brought me here. Some random act after a day of whiskey and a lifetime of failure to thrive? Or something planned and sinister; something rehearsed and well given to aforethought? The Universe deals such strange hands. It all appears random from a certain point.

I remember the wounded rabbit screaming in ungodly fear and pain. It is a high-pitched screeching sound, like that from an air-horn. You never expect such a horrible sound coming from such a small animal. You hear it for miles. The family of that rabbit certainly did. It is wounded, and I am drunk. My accomplices egg me on to finish it off with my .410 shotgun. I don't hesitate. I pull the trigger, and a life ends. The blood, fur, and sinew splatter. Only two mangled feet remain, nothing else is recognizable. Such random violence.

We are at a bifurcation. He now presses the gun against my temple. Like floating out in the middle of one of the marked lanes of the lake. The white floats bobbing up and down. The lanes are not clear from here; nothing has any symmetry. Hunter now rabbit. I will end up dead… or not. I finally just shrug. I give up. I fully capitulate. The grave fear dissipates as soon as I let go. Without a yin, there is no yang. Somehow the wild-man senses the relief of tension. He backs away and moves into the night. I breathe. We drive off.

We laugh the laugh of survivors and drive back to the Holiday Inn retelling the story. It is a way to scrub away the fear. I shake it off. Seemingly invincible, I sleep well that night. Years later I see the white floats in the middle of the lake and wonder how deaths and callings, like all boundary points, are arranged in such seemingly random fashion. I am amazed at how full of violence I was. How easy to channel that aggression in those days into some-

thing destructive. I suspect the man with the .45 felt the same. I was a breath away from being blown to pieces.

True callings, like this transgender process, can awaken in us a new way of seeing the markers. All I had to do was to survive the ignorance and darkness in myself and, a gun in my face, to find a symmetry in the patterning of the floats. With it comes a resolve to help others see that coherent linkage. It has taken so much randomness and violence to awaken in me even the possibility of such a sacred geometry. But, now I know for certain that those boundaries can become so very clear.

Somehow, knowing just now that the floats are not placed at random reduces the lostness I feel. It is so odd how that lessens the rage and fear. It creates in me the hope to live into my own becoming and amplifies the calling to teach the lesson to others.

Fatal Darkness

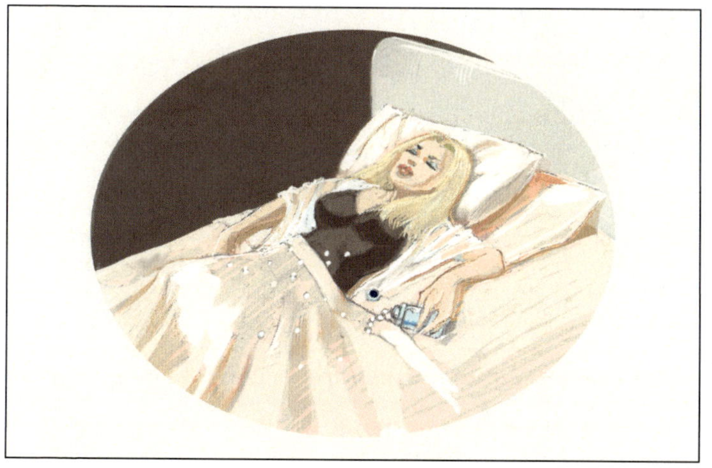

> *"No man, for any considerable period, can wear one face to himself and another to the multitude, without finally getting bewildered as to which may be the true."*
>
> —NATHANIEL HAWTHORNE

Quite recently, I realized that I once attempted suicide. I did not think much about it at the time, and perhaps it was just a suicide "gesture". But the thoughts and mechanics were there. Until I began to

honestly and relentlessly review my life and to look for anything related to being transgender, it was buried deep in my memories.

I think back to that weekend. It is the late part of winter, after Christmas break. Everything is grey and brutally cold: the weather, buildings, uniforms. It is "Gloom Period". There are two months until the apple blossoms explode and the blatant beauty of spring showers the upper Hudson Valley. Only four months till I graduate. Four months. But, I am in a deep funk that I cannot shake, and I cannot explain.

I am relentlessly devoted to being a cadet. This *is* who I am. In four years at West Point, I will have two dates, will never go to a movie on a weeknight, and rarely on weekends. It is a waste of my time. There is always work to do. Most nights for four years, I eat, come back to my room, sit at my desk, study, shine shoes, clean brass, get ready for the next morning. I am graded in each course most days. Grades are posted nightly. Day or night I can, and do, see where I rank in each. There is order in this world of mine. What is the pay-off? Recognition and affirmation. Yes, in this way I find a persona. I *am* what I *do*. It is a mask, but I cannot grasp that. I am too invested in the process.

Four months from the biggest moment in my life and I can find no contentment. I am bewildered. Irritable, restless, discontent, I harass plebes unmercifully to vent a volatile temper that simmers. I run miles to shed some pent up energetic. What fuels this rage? What am I hiding?

I feel broken in some existential way. Nothing fits. I am getting tired. It is a fatigue of the soul and spirit of which I know little. I soldier on living behind a persona I work very hard to modulate.

I have a weekend pass and want nothing more than to be alone. I can and do think about my life at these brief intervals of respite. It is the only time I give to introspection. Why can't I have a true relationship with others? I don't know. Why don't I have a girlfriend? I find no answers. Am I gay? Not likely, as I am not attracted to males. How does any of this work? I just don't know. Fuck it!

It is a dangerous feeling. I do not know what to do, but I feel a need to hide, to be by myself. Anyplace. I take a cab to the Holiday Inn at Newburgh. It is a clean and well-lighted place. I go to the convenience store next door, buy some cigarettes, and a Playboy. I walk across the street to get a hamburger at the Burger King. Cigarettes, a hamburger, a Playboy, and a place to be alone. With such comfort items, I can hide out for thirty-six hours. From what, I am not certain.

For some reason, it is the drawings of the Vargas women in the "gentleman's magazine" that generate the greatest response. They are incredibly beautiful, so lovely, so feminine. I find such deep comfort there. The bodies are symmetrical, sexy, perfect. I realize I *want something that they have. I want to be what they are.* I can never get there: sanitized, twisted, and projected, the aloneness

satisfies nothing. There is a deep hunger needing to be fed. But, I am cut off from my own interior and lost.

There is a five-hundred-word paper for a political science course that must be completed. It is an easy elective; not something esoteric nor difficult. I have to get something coherent down on paper and turn in on Monday. I have done this scores of times in the last thousand days. But, it is late on a Saturday night, and I am so far out of touch. I will soon graduate, am slated to spend the next three years as a paratrooper, and yet, I feel as if I am in Purgatory.

I work on the paper. Nothing sounds right. I start over. And over. And over. It gets worse and worse. I feel more distant and increasingly numb. I am just so tired of trying. It gets close to midnight. I am exhausted. Too tired to sleep, one thought emerges: "I just want to die." I am serious. Very, very serious. I run through my options: there is no gun, I have nothing good to hang myself with. What can I take? The idea of taking aspirin comes to me. I have read of such overdoses. I just want some relief.

I go to the all-night store. The clerk gives me an odd look. I buy several bottles of Bayer. I run back to the room. Not caring about outcome, I take several hands full. I lay back on the bed. I look at the ceiling. I am tired and out of sync with most everything. There is something pressing and deep, but it just won't come. *I am lost*!

Years later, I see an aspirin overdose while rounding in the Intensive Care Unit. It is not a common way to

commit suicide, maybe fifty a year die in this manner in the U.S. With enough ingestion, not much more than I took that night, there is a stimulation of the central respiratory drive leading to hyperventilation. There is a loss of potassium and bicarbonate in the urine. The symptoms: increasing respiratory rate and urine output. Kidneys fail, the heart loses rhythm, the risk of death is high. I experience these things as I lay on the bed. I am confused, my stomach upset, I cannot stop my rapid breathing. I get up to urinate again and again. It burns worse and worse. More than anything I feel sad and tired. I panic. In this fog, I think: I should call a cab and get back to safety. I don't want to die alone.

When I get back, it is very late and my roommate wonders at my return. I am not well. I go to bed. I hyperventilate and get up to pee repeatedly. Years later, I realize how close I have come to catastrophe. If I had told others what I had done, they would have forced me to go to the hospital. They would have checked me in, started I.V. therapy, and done a gastric lavage with liquid charcoal. Possibly, I would not have been able to graduate. I understand that so clearly now.

So, I have come from a dark place. I know the topography. Lost in the fragile land of ego, nothing makes sense. Fatigue and chaos are constants. It is a place of desperation, where needs despite all effort, cannot be satisfied. This is hell.

In my medical training, I love psychiatry. I flirt with the

idea of making it my specialty. It does not take me being well trained to know: I have survived a nervous breakdown, a psychic break. I was so very close to disaster. But, the real and important question still remains: what fueled the angst that erupted that desperate Saturday night? It will be years before I am introduced in my medical training to Maslow's "Theory of Need" hierarchy. It states that physiological needs are the most basic of the physical requirements for human survival. Unmet, the human body does not function properly. It fails to grow. These needs include breath, water, food, sleep, clothing, shelter, and sexual instinct. The last includes gender and sexual preference issues. Walled off and kept in the remote places of the psyche, these unidentified needs fuel a dangerously fulminant and primitive power. Erupting in so many lives without definition or exploration, they become fatal trip wires to psychic landmines. I am fortunate to have had protection and great fortune to get past the ignorance and the self-harm I initiated. I am a survivor.

I know others who were not so lucky. Charlie was a classmate and good friend at West Point. We room together as plebes. He commits suicide in early 2007. On a winter afternoon in Oklahoma, he pulls off the side of the road, walks out into a barren cotton field, puts a gun to his head, and shoots himself. Charlie was gay. He comes to terms with that years after graduation. Divorcing his wife, whom I know, he leaves behind two adult children. I meet them both when I give his eulogy at the

class memorial service at Arlington Cemetery. They are lovely people. Kind and earnest. They cannot understand so many aspects of this death. They cannot fathom how lost he was. "Sometimes, people get to a point where they are just tired," I say. It is inadequate, but the truth. Charlie teaches me something with his suicide. Having passed over the same abyss which dragged him under, his voice echoes a reminder: the only real requirement to truly live is to honor one's own integrity.

I know now after much exploration: I am a transgender woman. I have some functional tools for survival. The dark places in my journey I use as reminders of what could have been. I take my estrogen, do deep breathing, meditate, walk, drink water. But, the greatest irony is this: one day each week, I council people wrestling with issues of gender exploration. Many, like me, have wandered at an early point in the journey so very close to the edge of a deep chasm that could have swallowed them completely. I leave that clinic each week with a feeling of nourishment and contentedness. It is something rich and comes from deep within. In this way, I am feeding my own soul. It feels good and clean. And, when I get home, I look in the mirror. I am astonished: there is no mask.

That Day in Hammelburg

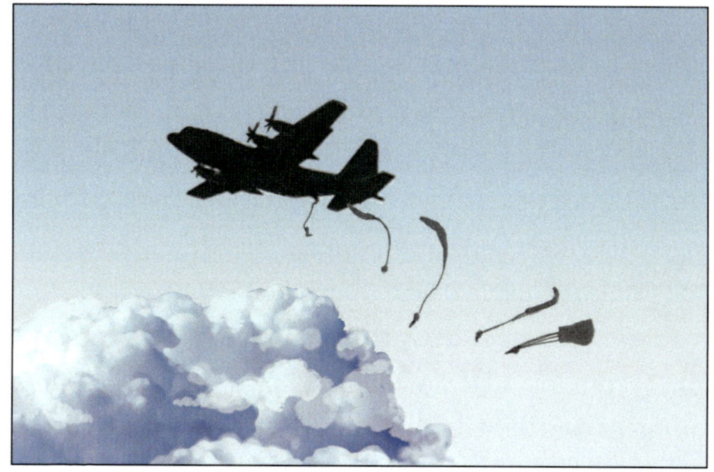

"And if only we arrange our life in accordance with the principle which tells us that we must always trust in the difficult, then what now appears to us as the most alien will become our most intimate and trusted experience."

—RAINER MARIA RILKE

When I was young, I was a paratrooper. I did jump school at Ft. Benning when I was still in school; then, on to the Infantry Officer Basic Course and Ranger school after graduation. In early 1974, I flew to Italy to join a unique airborne unit attached to NATO. It was magical. I think now about how vested I was in living as warrior. Perhaps I bonded so deeply to that masculine venue to damper the feminine that desperately wanted attention. Maybe. But I know this: I was always surrounded by so many good, honest people.

There really is a "brotherhood of arms". It is ancient and real. Picture the few surviving veterans from King Pyrrhus' army that won the battle against the Romans at Heraclea in 280 B.C. They lost lots of friends and brothers in that bloody exchange. Many years later, most of them were still closer to the memories of that time of trial than to family. If you have been there, you know how it is.

I am ashamed to say that I hated to see Nixon sign the accord to end the Vietnam War. I was young, naive, arrogant, and thought that it was my given right to go into combat. I see so much wrong with that. Now.

Back then, at best I thought I was invincible; that age seems to demand it. At worst, I was just dumb. Believe it or not, military school did not inflate that hubris. I did that on my own. Lord, no one hated war worse than some of the men who returned from two tours in Vietnam to teach at West Point. They had seen the sovereign grist of death on the battlefield. Strong men. I knew of a captain who was

an instructor. He could not wait to get out of the service. He would tell "war stories" at steak night on Wednesdays to entertain the upperclassman. But, mostly he was quiet. He wore one ribbon. The "Medal of Honor". That is *the* red badge of courage. None bigger. No one gets that without confronting a massive wall of trauma and chaos. Death, ambiguity, pain, and the utter randomness of the battle-field. I don't know if he ever reconciled the experience. In retrospect, he might have worn the ribbon to honor the ones that did not come back. It could have been an odd antidote to "survivor's guilt". Fact was: he had seen death and smelled it. His own. Having survived, more than forty years later it would not be odd if he still ponders.

How could I have been so blind? Every day of those four years on the Hudson taps was played to honor a fresh death in the killing fields. My roommate's father died our senior year. He was the last general killed in the war. It hit my friend hard. He carried a grudge the years he had to serve. He hated that his father had been sacrificed. The paradox was that the father was doing exactly what he felt called to do. I know now that there is justice deep in that construct. After surviving long years of trauma inherent in my doctoring career, I now think of the loss of humanity. But, for those who model the true warrior archetype, it is not so clear. There are things worth dying for. Warriors, true ones, flush with integrity, honor their paths the best they can. I knew many of those men. For them, death was simply an acceptable risk.

I have strayed far from intent. I want to honor the death of two young paratroopers, Mike Rohrer and Charlie Capps. They were two men who died in peacetime. There is some special irony for those killed in the line of duty but not in war. I am saddened by the untimeliness and misfortune of their demise. It still rankles me.

But, there were two men that died in Hammelburg, Germany one bright July morning in 1976. I was there. They were good soldiers. Well thought of. One was the colonel's driver. The other in Alpha Company. They were young, tough kids. They thought nothing of drinking local wine till 5:00 am, then running five miles in Physical Therapy at 6:00 am, then doing a full day's work. They were the type of men/boys you played high school football with, who carried your mother's groceries to the car. The ones who dated your sister and you didn't mind.

I can still see parts of that day in clear tones. Like an old Polaroid under the glass on my desk. This dreary time of the year it still comes and sits with me. My unit was stationed in Italy. We were part of the NATO "Ace Mobile Force". Each country had a small unit in this "elite" group. Most were paratrooper units. We did lots of traveling to exotic places to jump out of airplanes. We trained in Germany, jumped in Great Britain, ran patrols in Turkey, survived in Belgium Commando School. It was a hell of a good time.

It was peacetime. No one thought much about dying in battle. All of us talked about "the balloon going up"

which was a metaphor for an all-out war with the Soviet Union. At that point, deep in the Cold War, the Red Army was our nemesis. All strategy focused on what to do when thousands of tanks came screaming down the Fulda Gap in eastern Germany. We just knew it would happen. We even hoped it would. And *then*, we would be in the middle of what we all craved: combat. "In contact" was the descriptive. Fighting and defending what we thought was good and true.

It was much later that I learned that our real mission was terribly dangerous. We were the ones tasked to establish an airhead. That is the location where everyone else would land. Given the nature of the conventional war that was anticipated, casualties among the first combatants would be massive. Given that mission, our chances of short term survival were slender at best.

The NATO relationships were odd from a military perspective. We were stationed in Italy to "show the flag". We did field exercises, however, in large training areas in Germany. Two or three times a year, we would load up all equipment, then fly into or "jump" into Hohenfels, Wildflecken, or Grafenwohr. People wonder how armies learn how to make war. Fire teams, squads, platoons, companies, battalions, brigades, divisions, they practice. Repeatedly. That's how it's done. It is expensive. It requires infinite planning and patience. But, that is how, at least in the old days, liberty was defended.

Hammelburg is located east of Frankfurt near Bad

Kissingen. Surrounded by a thick ancient forest, it was used as a POW camp for captured Allied army personnel. It was a living hell for those soldiers who were imprisoned there. Some had been marched there from the Battle of the Bulge. Five hundred miles through snow in the middle of winter. Survivors were not numerous. Bad karma and all, after the war, the base became a training station. It was a staging area for U.S. and NATO troop movement. An exercise like that brought us there that fated day.

It had taken the better part of a week to get all gear and personnel from Aviano, Italy to Wildflecken. I had been on leave in the States just before. It was my first trip back home in over a year and I was still wrestling with jet lag. I was in the last group to move up and was on the ground for the jump as a member of the drop zone cadre.

There is an orchestrated, violent beauty to a military jump. The ritual begins with picking up a chute from the "riggers". These men are the ones that spend their days repacking the chutes after a jump. Lives depend on this learned skill. After the chutes are handed out, platoons cluster. Each troop helps another don the gear. It's like wearing a very heavy life preserver. There are preliminary checks by squad leaders, then again by the platoon sergeant. Each buckle and harness is inspected. Not just looked at, *examined*. Any fray, twist, or broken buckle and the chute is discarded. We then sit on the ground in rows like a gaggle of term pregnant women. We hurry up, then we wait. It is the Army way. Then the jumpmasters

begin. Most are hardened veterans, savvy commissioned and non-commissioned officers, who have done this a hundred times. But, they all treat it like it was the first... or the last. Care and safety with dangerous and serious men.

Before loading, the jumpmaster's briefing is given. Every detail of safety, hand signals for types of duress, and commands are covered as if we have never heard them before. Small groups then stand up. The tail of the C-130 can drop down like the jaw of a great steel dragon. Into the yawning cavern waddle the warriors. The jumpmaster, acting like a maitre'd at a fine restaurant, leads each of four single files or "sticks" into the bowels from the rear of the aircraft. In summer, it feels like a hot cave. Both sides of the interior have narrow, aluminum and canvas seats. These are mirrored in the center. Faces are now painted with camouflage. There is a constant, thunderous roar of the plane props now in motion. The noise drowns out everything except thought. Sixty soldier souls are packed into a small space. Nothing but deafening sound, like massive crashing waves in a hurricane. Maybe louder. It is constant. Each brother faces another; one cannot move. If you need to urinate you do it in your pants. The space in the aisles belongs only to the demigods; the jumpmasters prowl, ever vigilant.

Imagine a flying, prehistoric beast. Think of seeing a covey of these fierce looking alien life forms cresting over the horizon like revenging Valkyries. Terror in the skies. They are each the size of two and a half houses and the

width of a large porch. Flying like monstrous, mythical dragons they create a soft rumble like muffled thunder. As they loom closer, it crescendos. Louder. Louder. In the blink of an eye, the lumbering, pregnant beings float just over the clearing. From the ground looking up you see small dots then strange plumes streaming out of the bowels of these massive creatures. Hundreds of them. "Death from above" is our motto.

Back to the drama: the doors and rear of the aircraft slam closed. In the shady bowels, there is a focused, boiling, raging, chaos slowly building. Each locks into his own space. Some sleep, some silently sing, others zone out. The tension builds.

Then, it is time. Twenty minutes out, the pilot relays the plane's position through the jumpmaster's headset. The first jump sequence command is screamed out. "Twenty minutes!" Twenty minutes till we fall from six hundred feet. The troops now ramp up. There are some "hoo-hah's" and barking; then it settles again. Systole and diastole. Then the second jump command, "Ten minutes!" It evokes some random screaming and bizarre profanity. Then, it becomes real: the doors open. Think of standing next to a railroad track as a thundering train screams by. That's the sound. If it's cold, like night jumps in the middle of winter, the wind cuts like a sharp razor. All part of the ritual.

With the next command, things begin to go faster. "Six minutes!" is followed immediately by "Get ready!"

The light by the door turns on. Bright red. The energy mushrooms. It is palpable. Grown men in a frenzy, are nearing a peak. Then, "Outboard personnel stand up!" Those near the skin of the craft stand. "Inboard personnel stand up!" Now, "Hook up!" The jumpers, each holding a clip in hand, connect to the static line. The large snap-link anchors the parachute to a thick wire that runs the length of the aircraft. By jumping out, gravity and speed open the canopy. No thinking required. Just get to the door. Jump up and out. Up and out.

"Check static lines!" Everyone checks that the life line is not tangled and is securely fastened. "Check equip-ment!" Each looks one final time at their gear and at the back of the troop just in front. It is the last chance to make sure nothing is out of order. "Sound off for equipment check!" The jumper just behind the man nearest the door shouts, "OK!" if all is kosher with the equipment of the man in front of him. The "OK's" echo to the last man in the stick, who looks at the jumpmaster, points, and screams, "All OK!"

There is a time lapse between the final "All OK" and the next command. It can last a minute or longer. It is the time when the door is open, the red light on, and the adrenaline is gushing. We are nearing a climax. It is a moment many of us look back on with such fondness; I am young and feel so alive. The future is a jumbled matrix. What matters is right in front of me. How magical; it is a point where I am fully present to my own life.

"Stand in the door!" It is just seconds away. As the jumpmaster screams this out, he slaps the first man on the back. Excitement, fear, anticipation, crescendo as he scoots to a position with hands braced just outside the door. There is something very special about being the first "man in the door". During that pregnant period when the light is red your hands feel the vibration of the massive flying machine, you look down at the earth flying by, and you feel like a powerful and invincible god. For the briefest moment, it all slows down. There is no way to convey the overwhelming and mystical sentience of that sliver in time.

Then, the light flashes green. No thinking. Just reaction. Up and out. Up and out. Just like the first jump at Benning. Get up and out. The static line extends, out comes the chute. It's so very quiet. One second I am standing by a screaming train, the next, it is as quiet as if I am alone in my bed. I hear the voices of other jumpers. Dogs, I can hear the dogs going crazy on the ground. There is the greatest relief, and I think one thing: "Fucking 'A'!"

I locate the colored smoke placed on the ground by the drop zone cadre. Six hundred feet goes fast. Nearing the ground. Pulling hard now on the left riser. I steer into the wind. Nearing the ground. Pull hard, pull hard. The anterior lip of the chute lifts. Whoosh! Plop! A good soft landing. An orgasm. Hit, do a parachute landing fall, stop. Get up, collapse the chute. Roll it up. Find where you are. Where your men are. Training jumps are one thing,

but, with tracers and machine gun fire, that lazy time in the air is hell. Fifty per cent death rates and higher were common with jumps in WWII. That was before they even hit the ground.

This is the narrative of what that day at Hammelburg should have been. It was the story of my sixty-nine jumps. It was the mantra of the collective jumps of thousands of modern paratroopers. We marshaled at Wildflecken. The planes took off, flew forty kilometers south. It was a bright, clear day in July. Wind speed was not high. It was not humid, and conditions on the Drop Zone were good. For landing, there were wide, clear fields, no ground cover except thick grass, and relatively soft ground. During the short flight, they went through the standard commands, then jumped.

This is where something goes terribly wrong. How I saw it from the ground: the planes are in trail. The ribbons of opening chutes fill the sky. But, from the third bird back something hurdles to the ground. It looks, from where I am, like a chute on a piece of equipment. It comes down with violence, speed, and force.

I know this. When something completely catastrophic happens, the mind can refuse to compute. In years of jumps, I never saw a chute fail to open properly. Ever. When a chute wraps around a jumper, he's a dead man. And the mechanics to cause such a thing are, at best, remote. Odds: thousands and thousands to one. But, others nearby see it happening. In the seconds that I hear

shouts of "pull your reserve, pull your reserve" it registers. This is a paratrooper falling to his death.

In the U.S. Army, in the best units, deadly crisis brings out steady calm in the professionals. This is what we do. My platoon sergeant and the drop zone safety officer are close to the impact. They rush over. I hear one of them say, "Oh my God. There's two of them." Two men, not one, have plunged to their death. A twisted lump. Tangled together, in some horrible and bizarre fatal dance of Fate. Years later, someone said that they remember the perfect circle of blood and fluids which ring the impact area. Thirty feet in diameter. The cadre seals off the area. They call for the Medivac. People do their jobs.

Word spreads like a raging fire. "Who was it?" "Oh shit, oh shit!" "Who bit?" "No fucking way!" There are some moans, and a few sobs. Some drop to their knees to pray. For a minute: chaos. Then order. Teams go to rally-points. Squads link up. Platoons make head counts. In short order, it is known by subtraction who has gone down. The paradox: in time of war, two casualties in a combat jump is a miracle. Secure the bodies, move on. This is not combat. No one expects such blunt trauma. It is so... unfair. So... wrong. This just can't be.

Colonel Dean Darling is the commander. He is nearly six-foot-tall, with grey bushy, short cropped hair. His nose and Adam's apple out of proportion to an honest, angular face. He talks in a clipped sort of way. Barks a sentence; left face, stop, sentence. He won my confidence that day.

Handled a shitty, shitty hand like a wise leader should. He tells us who has died. Nothing yet is clear about the why. He is honest. He acknowledges the grief and disbelief. He has the chaplain pray. Things calm a bit. He then gets back up and says this, "We will not rest until we jump again. We will march back to Wildflecken; the riggers will repack our chutes. We will get back in those C-130's in the morning and do what we are paid to do." It is twenty-five miles back as the crow flies. Thirty by the route we take. It is mid-afternoon by the time we have a prayer service and complete the order of march.

We begin. I remember that it felt mostly like a dark dream. At this early point, it still does not register. I see the road, hear the troops talking softly, feel the cool as the sun sets. By then, like most, I am zoned out. Present, not present. We head into the woods. Each person now deep in his own thoughts. Very little talk. We stop for water and sometime after midnight we eat rations that we carry. From that point on, I have jumbled memories of the next five hours. The shadows and moon light filter through the high branches, causing ebb and flow of unearthly patterns. It is like a fever dream, but the smells and crackling of footsteps on the forest floor are just enough to prevent one from going completely into an altered state. I cannot say that we were not on the interface of some mystical realm that whole night. There are points where I could swear that I could have walked into another world, but as the morning light slowly rises, those shadows and strange

boundaries are gone. I am miserably sore. So tired. But it doesn't register in the normal way my body processes. This is another man walking. Not me. It is another life in which something tragic and unexplainable has happened. Not mine. This could not be me, it could not be my life. This is not happening.

Years later I think back on that march. Each of us who went through it were altered in some ill-defined way. There are no words to adequately describe the feeling, but, I know for certain, that I felt much older when the sun came up on the horizon the next morning. I lost an innocence in that long night.

It is a cloudy day. There are some scattered rain clouds building in the distance. All of us are jumpy, all dead tired; but, we are strangely focused. We do the jump sequence, load, fly back, and jump. There is mostly silence in those spots where chaos and screaming always prevail. An exit out that door offers us each a gift: catharsis. It is the final prayer of a ritual pilgrimage honoring our two dead comrades. It is fitting tribute in the warrior way.

Piecing together what happened in the plane that day was never easy. Urban legend took over immediately after it happened. It appears that either Capps or Rohrer was early in the stick. For some unknown reason, he did not get a good exit from the door. Anathema to all paratroopers: there is a hung jumper. That means the man is tied to the plane. The chute does not fully deploy. The jumpmaster sees the static line bow. He leans out and looks to

confirm. It is a textbook response. But in this time, two or three jumpers continue out the door, unaware of the drama unfolding. The hung jumper is not conscious. He is not responding to the jumpmaster's hand signal. Before anything else can be done, the second in the doomed pair jumps. Again, the odds of poor exit and hung jumper are so very, very, very small. One jumper in a hundred thousand and it happens twice in one stick of fifteen men. Rough odds: ten billion to one. 10,000,000,000 to 1.

There is a second bizarre and tragic occurrence: the angle of each hung jumper is such that as one swings toward the aircraft tail he slams against the plane and ricochets back like a ball on a tether. The odds are insanely low of one jumper hitting the moving target that is the other. But, the two young men hit squarely face to face. There is enough force with the violent contact to snap the static lines. These lines are tested to thousands of pounds of tensile strength. They never, ever snap. The odds of it happening: slim and none. The lines then whip around the two like the cord from a spool. They are instantly enshrouded in the canopy trying to unfurl. Someone said they thought one gained enough consciousness to try and pull the reserve. I did not see that. I hope not, because it would have been the last several seconds of a life, and it would have been full of great terror. It is something that I hope never to know.

So, in the blinking of an eye, two good men die. That has been forty-two years ago this summer. I heard later

that the locals erected a monument in memoriam. I hope it is true. But, for me, I still carry a fragment of that odd and fatal day deep in my bones. All of us who walked through the primeval forests that long night suffered deep wounds that are not seen but are felt at the core of our being. There is a song that resonates with what I learned that fatal day:

"Let me watch my children grow
To see what they become
Lord, don't let that cold wind blow
'Til I'm too old to die young
I have had some real good friends
I thought would never die
But all I've got that's left of them
Are these teardrops in my eye."

—JOHN HADLEY

Family, Fishing, Leaving Home, and Other Chaotic Things

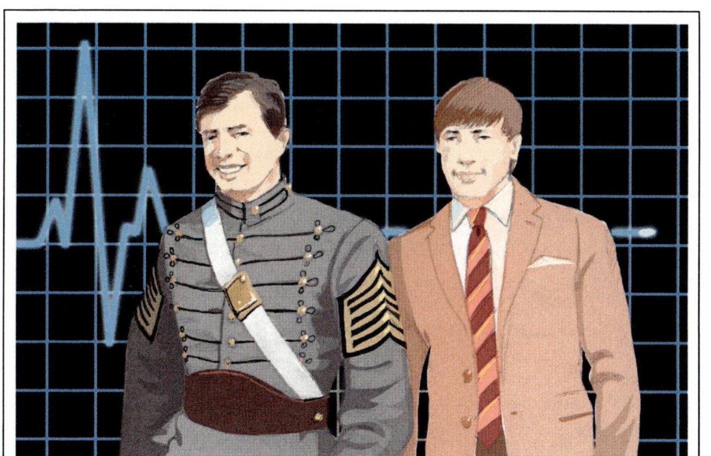

"*In all chaos there is a cosmos, in all disorder a secret order.*"

—CARL JUNG

Today, I remember a late July morning in 1978 on the banks of the Brazos River. Iredell, Texas is the epicenter of my clan. It is in Central Texas, ninety miles south of Ft. Worth. It is a simple gas stop now, on Highway 6, between Stephenville and Waco. My people have roots and stories here. Like the day one hundred years before, when an Army Air Corps bi-plane takes my grandfather, Jack, handsome and jaunty as a movie star, away to become a full-fledged myth. John Oliver, his given name, is the first of only a few who train others in the art of flying during World War I. These flying machines are simple constructs of wood with struts, wire, and leather pieced together with an ingenuity that mock the earth they leap from.

In those days, people live such close-knit and sheltered lives. I wonder what his mother might have said to him at the breakfast table that morning. There is no reference point; nothing to warn away, nothing to give motherly advice about. That is the crucial element. For on that special day, Jack forever inducts my tribe into a future that is chaotic and far removed from the ice cream socials and rituals of small town USA. It makes little difference that he will lose those hard-earned wings for zooming under tall bridges. No matter what comes later, he has honored a calling that will cause a ripple of transformation in his life and in those of generations to come. Years later, when he is laying on his deathbed, I cannot understand why my favorite person in the world is confined to rest instead of

going fishing with me. Dozens of times in my young life we have done so. I see his big grin. He smiles most of the time, even at the end.

I think back and hope he remembered how much joy he felt on that day he took off from Iredell and on those lovely days we went fishing. A grocer man by trade, he could do electrical work, plumbing, carpentry. He was handy. He was happy. He ventured outside of suffocating boundaries and found great joy in living. In doing so, he opened the door for others of us to go through. I understand that now.

But, on that July 1978 day, just a long baseball throw aimed to the west of that bridge my grandfather flew over, my brother and I are exploring. For a time in our lives, fishing is something that we both love to do together. It keeps us close. It is the one thing that we have in common. The simple ritual of making time, getting our gear together, finding bait, driving, smoking Marlboro's, talking about the Dallas Cowboys, and our parents. There is a calm and reverence to the communications and a real sense of bonding. I just assume it will always be like this. But as we grow older, I find I am more rigid. I simply lose interest. Life and addiction get in the way for many years. It is a small miracle that he seems to love me anyway. He is the first to accept my transgender exploration.

Nine years apart, he is the younger. Growing up, he is always around. That is fine most of the time, but, it is not seemingly healthy for him. I sneak him into the ini-

tial screening of "The Exorcist". It is one of the scariest movies ever made. The extreme horror and graphic terror scar him. He does not sleep without the light on for years. He comes to Italy each year for Christmas when I am a paratrooper there. Somewhere I have a picture of him being carried under one arm by a large German fraulein in Munich. She serves us beer after beer in large liter steins. The under-arm ride is free. Of course, he is under age.

They are distant and random things, but because of me, he grows up with distorted images of what maturity entails. It fosters a false bravado and a distancing, at an early point, from heart-centered living. I know that only in retrospect, but it does not negate a central fact: he carries trauma inflicted by someone close to him. Those were fun days in an odd sort of way, but within the psyche, it is still friendly fire. I see that now, and it makes me sad.

But, on that sweet July day, we find a tributary of the episodic Brazos River that has been formed by a late May deluge. There are pools the size of small houses that dot the river bed. With a cane pole and small hooks, we lure bass the size of our arms out of that water. It is magical to drop still squirming earthworms into the reflecting pool and seconds later watch the red and white bob get yanked under. We scream and pull hard. Then, those large creatures with such great energy and vigor, twist, turn, grapple, and flop in a final attempt to go back to a place called home. Their eyes are full of amazement. They seem stunned by the violence of their own process.

I see the same look in a patient's eyes in an Emergency Room years later. A man I don't know is having a heart attack. I am an intern, and new to the frenzy that always seems to stir in this area of the large hospital. I help a paramedic transfer the man to a gurney. When I ask one of the other medics who has watched the cardiac monitor on the ambulance ride in, he just says, "bad chest pain," and stiffly shakes his head. It is not a good sign. He knows, and I learn, this is fatal. In a brief flash, though, I see in that man's eyes something that looks like the innocent wonder and unadulterated amazement I see in the soft eyes of my grandfather laying on the hospital bed, and also, in the eyes of the fish that summer morning in Iredell. I don't know for certain, but, perhaps, leaving home for good registers that way in all of God's creatures.

My Dad

Teach your parents well,
Their children's hell will slowly go by,
And feed them on your dreams
The one they pick, the one you'll know by.
Don't you ever ask them why, if they told you, you will cry,
So just look at them and sigh, and know they love you.

—GRAHAM NASH

My father died of a gunshot wound to the head in 2003. I am laying on a sofa in a small suite at La Posada in Santa Fe, New Mexico. The soft light of the ending of a beautiful spring day filters through the curtains. I am watching my beloved Dallas Stars play Edmonton in a first-round Stanley Cup hockey game. I hear the phone ring. It is my brother. We are very close, but we do not call without intent.

"Bro, Luigi has gone down," he says with a broken voice. It is a simple statement, but for years, one I dread hearing. I sit for several seconds and do not want to pro-

cess or move. Luigi is the affectionate nickname we use for my father. After the advent of *The Godfather* movies, we always saw him in the Marlon Brando role. Thus, "Don Luigi" was created. I finally answer, "What do you mean?" My brother then says, "It looks like he shot himself."

My father was a good man. He was a long time independent grocer man who had what one Methodist minister called, "the gift of the host." Biblically, that meant that he was unselfish and went the extra mile to help others to feel at home.

I remember a Christmas morning that he asks me to go with him to the store. It is the only day of the year that it is closed. He rarely asks me to do such things, and I think it odd, but I go without question. We go to the large refrigerated locker and there are twenty fully prepared turkey and dressing dinners from the store's steam table. Then we spend the morning going unannounced to different houses. He knows who can use some help and right where each one lives. One of my dialysis patients opens her door sheepishly when we knock. She and a small son have been huddling under blankets in a leaky, poorly shingled, shotgun house. A candle is burning for heat. They have a pitiful six-inch plastic tree to honor Santa's visit. There are no lights. We leave enough food to last a week. True to form, my Dad finds a way to slip a twenty-dollar bill to the sobbing mother.

His best friend was a general contractor and a World Champion rodeo cowboy. He was tough as nails, and never

asked for any help. But, early in her life, his eighteen-year-old daughter made some poor life choices. He came to have coffee with my father and told him that he thought that the girl had run off to California. It was one of the busiest times of the summer, but my father said, "Let's go get her." Ten days later they were all home. The girl later became a nurse, and always gave my father credit for directing that unselfish rescue. That was my Dad.

I remember when my grandfather died. He was my father's mentor and best friend. Jack had smoked since he was eight. When lung cancer showed up at fifty-six, he went down quickly. He left behind an oil drilling company that owed hundreds of thousands of dollars after a series of dry holes. The brothers, most with their own alcohol-related issues, declined to help pay the debt. My Dad would not allow his father's name to be tarnished. He went to everyone he knew and pledged repayment of those loans. He worked night and day for years, but everyone got what was due. His name was synonymous with trust in that small town.

Ultimately, he created a thriving business out of that store. After my mother died, he turned down an offer to sell it for over six million dollars. He said it was not enough money to sell a thing he so dearly loved. He did not want to give it up. Several months later a large chain moved in, and the value plummeted to nothing. Later on, he struggled with the bank, debt, and resources, but, he never complained about it while alive. After his

death, my brother and I did as instructed. We flew to Italy and spread his ashes in Lake Como. At the end of the ritual we turned to the west and lifted our middle fingers. We chanted in unison, "From Don Luigi: Fuck all the bankers!"

The day my mother died, he cried inconsolably. I was hungover and he watched the death of his best friend with only two nurses to bear witness. He was predictably trying to call friends to console them when I found him. But his wailing was uncontrollable. I just hugged him while we both sobbed. Although he tried, he was never the same. The money ran thin, and he got tired. I had a certain premonition that something bad was going to happen in his life the coming year, so I went with him to New York City for Christmas in 2002. I did not have the cash nor time, but I was certain that it was the right thing to do. We stayed at the Waldorf Astoria and had dinner at Tavern on the Green. He spent quality time with me and others. The 26th of December, the anniversary of my mother's death, we hired a limo to take us up the Henry Hudson Parkway to West Point. Although I was the one who graduated there, he always deeply loved the place. He was so proud that one of his own had gone there. We walked the grounds, we did small talk, we told each other stories, and we listened to the joy and sadness of the other. By the end of the long day, as he lay sleeping in the back of that car, I looked on a face finally filled with some peace. We had shared what fathers and sons are supposed to share, at

a time of great unction. He was dead three months later, but we had said all that was needed.

I remember the last time I saw him. I had come a hundred miles south to see patients. We had coffee at his house. It was a special space full of all of the memorabilia from a life of travel and reading. He was the only person I ever knew who read the Encyclopedia Britannica like a book. As we talked that day, he smiled that loving smile and I saw in those beautiful eyes some deep tenderness that I thought had somehow vanished. He came out front to hug me and watch me drive off. I looked in my mirror and saw a paradoxical smile on his face as he watched me turn the corner. It was a smile of pride, and yet it was terribly sad too. I spilled coffee while watching him watch me, and drove back around. He had gone inside. When I knocked and asked him for a pair of his trousers, he was inexplicably brusque. The last time we hugged, I noted some resistance. He stiffened as I embraced him deeply. I thought there was something that I had done or something that was somehow inappropriate, but I could not figure what. Two weeks later he was gone.

The local judge and the police did a full investigation and ruled the death an accident. I am comfortable with that. But, what they did not know was that for several years my father had an insurance policy with his two sons as beneficiaries. We consoled him, when a year earlier, it was apparent that he could not fund the premiums. What we did not realize was that he sold everything he could to

extend the policy. Legally, that policy did not "end" the day my father died. However, one certainly could have interpreted it that way. It would not have been unreasonable to construct a scenario in which *he* believed that there were two hours left on those multi-million-dollar term life policies the night the "accident" happened. We will never know, but my Dad loved his boys and always wanted them to have the best. They always did.

The Oldest of the Girls

"Your potentials should become blessings to the earth, giving hope to people and solving the problems that you were born to solve, while you yourself go to the grave empty."

—CLEMENT OGEDEGBE

I watched one of the best men I ever knew die of Amyotrophic Lateral Sclerosis (ALS), Lou Gehrig's disease. It is a slow and horrible journey. For reasons unclear, nerve bundles that generate strength slowly decay. The voluntary muscles that control voice and breath shrink without stimulation. They become stiff and finally fail. Talking and breathing diminish, and in the end, there is silence and gasping.

My friend was a good man. The honest voice and unvarnished truth that he breathed into most any situation were so subtle that they almost felt too simple. But, his counsel and friendship were so consistent over such

long intervals, that it was obvious that it came from a deep, unviolated, and, heartfelt place. He wore a cape of innocence, which came from always thinking the best of people and situations. It was not naiveté, but an unshaken belief in the integrity of others. At times, people, including me, did not seemingly deserve that, but it was just who and what he was. He could not have changed that even if he had tried.

In the 1980's, he was the president of a large banking organization. It was a chaotic time in that business. Some of his acquaintances from that association were convicted of crimes, and went to jail. It was only in retrospect that we understood how significant his honesty was. I am certain that he was tempted to follow in the footsteps that led so many astray, but his honor and name were never tarnished. That was the type of man he was.

Such a sad paradox to watch him at the end slowly lose those things that made him so unique. But, like everything else in his life: he accepted what could not be changed, and he tried with great courage to alter the issues that were malleable. I was the one in recovery, but, he modeled the Serenity Prayer of Alcoholics Anonymous for me in a marvelous way. That prayer says, "God grant me the serenity to accept the things I cannot change; courage to change the things I can; and wisdom to know the difference."

The best thing was that he was innocent in a way that made him oblivious to his own authenticity. His was such an honest and simple integrity. He knew nothing different.

It just shined through in every relationship he had and in every position he ever held. He made it seem so simple and so matter of fact. It was not his intellect nor mantra that elevated his life; it was the constancy to the truths he lived into that made him such an unusual human.

Odd, but we never talked much about his past, nor very deeply about the ways that he understood the world. He was solitary in that way, but, he never met a stranger, and, by the end of his life, he had friendships all over the world. He was open and honest in his exchanges. They were never esoteric, but they were warm and heartfelt. He said what he meant, and meant what he said. It would be a mistake to label him as a simple man. There were complexities that existed, but he tended to share those only with his beloved wife, if he did with anyone.

In his maturity, he never inserted himself into the personal business of others. He knew that avoiding such treacherous terrain was the only way to maintain long term friendships. But, I know it took great restraint to stay aloof of some of those issues at times. If I have any regrets, it was that I did not ask him for advice enough. He was a bright, articulate man, who was a soldier, civic leader, husband, and father. Devout, he never preached nor cowed others who saw things differently. I wish now that I would have pried into the experiences that he had had, and sought his counsel on a variety of things, especially about money and resources. I always felt inferior to this man, and it bothers me that I see this only in retrospect.

He was a dedicated family man. That devotion created the opportunities for him to visit with his extended crew during Christmas, 4th of July, weeks in Mexico. They spent time together, and that was pure genius. Some way, he knew that time together created a fluency between members of a clan. It was a language that could, and would, be used in darker days to mend broken fences and to patch tattered dreams. By what I could tell, during those vacations he always chatted about current events, sports, even politics. I gather it was never about anything that was polarizing. But, in the end, it was never the things that were said, it was just that his people were present together. Amazingly, this most down to earth man taught me about the metaphysics of relationship.

He grew up in Oklahoma in an oil camp. His father was a journeyman who took care of business. Work was a way of life. His mother was the backbone of the family. She was educated, loving, but formal. She was the school principal in their small town when that meant something. She was strict but always seemed fair from a distance. With his mother's educational background, there was no doubt that he would go to college. When he did, he joined a fraternity. It was not the "Animal House" experience. These were the days of formal dining and of swearing an oath to a brotherhood. He dated the only woman he ever loved, who played in the band, and they just fit. They married, and seemingly, like all of his endeavors, it was just the next right thing to do.

I am sure that marriage was not as easy as they made it look in public. How did he and his mate handle aggression? That becomes a central question that must be answered for such relationships to age. We discussed this obliquely, but again, it was not what he said, it was always what he *did* that was significant. Interestingly, he channeled the aggression by projection. Whether it was tackling business deals, devoting energy to business club projects, the Dallas Cowboys, or politics, the tension was focused on something outside the container. The examples taught me this: energy showered on other issues beyond the boundaries of the home, dissipates the destructive passions. Given time, the relationship itself heals such ego derived issues. He knew that it was the love from the collective matrix of family that healed the individuated edges. Pure genius.

I have thought a great deal about what this man would think about my transgender issues. I have wished more than once that I could ask him what he would do. I know he would be honest. He was a Rotarian and was fanatic about showing up and being accountable. At his death, he had over forty-two years of consecutive meetings attended. 2,184 times he made room in a busy day, stopped what he was doing, wherever he was, and went to be one among others.

How odd, then, while walking one day recently I notice someone has put up a sign on the side of the road with "The Four-Way Test of Rotary". I cannot miss it. These are the tenets of the "Test" that club members are encouraged

to use in making life decisions. One, is it the truth? Two, is it fair to all concerned? Three, will it build goodwill and better friendships? Four, will it be beneficial to all concerned? There was his moral code staring at me. I have traveled far enough down my life path to know the utility of such a theorem. My friend loved the actor John Wayne, who reminded: "A man's got to have a code, a creed to live by, no matter his job." Seeing that sign, just when I did, was no coincidence. It is just another in a long line of gifts from a good man and a lovely friend.

When I apply The Four-Way Test to my current life I find these truths: I know who I am, what I am, and how I am called to serve. I am a transgender woman who is being asked to educate others about this process. Fairness is so relative; so, I do not know the answer to the second question any more than he did in contracting ALS. It did not appear fair for him to suffer in that way, but it was what he was given, and he made the best of it. I suspect that there are higher orders of truth where that type of question finds a resolution. But, I do know that the world needs good and solid people to live courageous lives, to break down barriers, to take odd situations and own them in heroic ways. That answers the third part. The fourth question will be answered only as I live into the journey ahead. It cannot be known in advance.

Many unusual things are being asked of me. How do I respond? How do I live? What should I do? In this journey among shadows and uncertainty, many things

are not clear. There is continuous shape-shifting, and most everything is uncertain. I seek help daily to ascertain a higher vision and path. In the midst of this drama, I frequently remember that I have been given gifts from Spirit that guide and shepherd me through these awkward times. One of those gifts involves this man and his death. In many native traditions, it is a belief that the dying impart a blessing to another as they leave. To be holding the hand of a leader as they move on is seen as a great honor. In this mystical exchange, there is a promise of protection and guidance.

Isn't it paradoxical, that out of everyone who could have been present in the room at the time that he died, I was there? I was the one who stood by the bedside and held his hand as my friend and mentor passed away. I certainly feel his guidance these days, and I am proud to say that I bear his legacy. I am truly the oldest of his girls and most blessed of the extended family that he left behind.

"Attitude is altitude!"

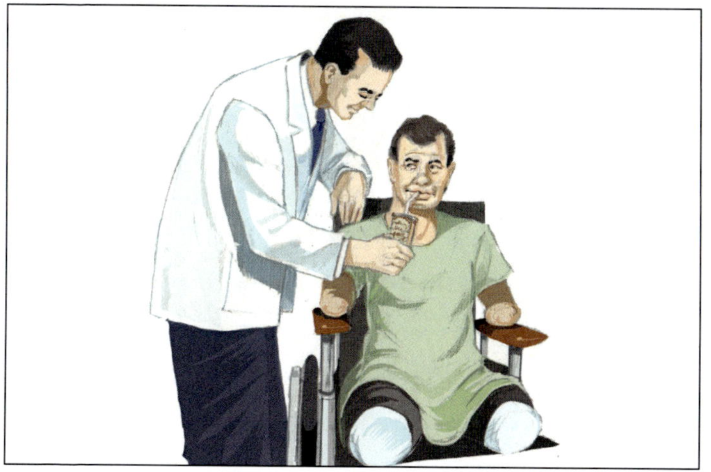

"*Courage is found in unlikely places.*"

—J.R.R. TOLKIEN

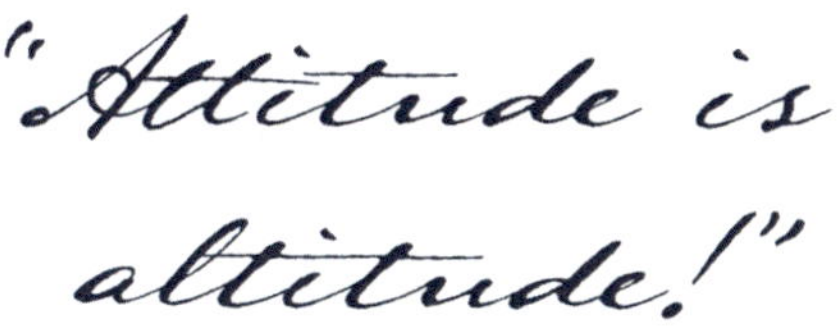

It is odd that later in life, great drama seems to have found me. My ego tells me this: it is not a good time. But then, that ego is seemingly the epicenter of my problems. Frequently, I feel deep sadness, a terror of the

unknown, and a general angst. This cannot be good. Or can it?

So often in the last twenty-five years of my life, I have been witness to ordinary humans showing super-human courage in such times of duress. The rote skill set that my medical training gave me to use in times of such perceived darkness was impotent in so many ways. It was in the most unusual and unexpected places I learned things of the heart that were more powerful. More useful. These teachings always came from learning at the hands of true masters. Who were these amazing beings? They were not brilliant professors nor affluent teachers; they were my patients.

I write in my journal in May 1994: "I can't explain it other than stating that sometimes things have a profound vibrance and clarity. It is not captured with physical sight, it is a truer vision, and it always seems to stem from something one of my patients has shown me. I had that sense today. That feeling of being in touch with an absolute certainty. When I looked into this older woman's eyes, there it was! It was truth reflected back to me. Neither of us "knew" anything about the construct, but both of us felt transformed and completely comfortable in some vital way."

These people were fluent in a language of the spirit that still mystifies, yet now really sustains me. I have been in recent funks, tough times, but these are the type of days that they taught me how to accommodate. I am not speak-

ing of a verbal communication skill set, but something more complex. I was terribly naive and arrogant when I first entered into that realm. Perhaps it was my parochial upbringing or some cultural residue, but I assumed that the plain lifestyles and circumstances of the ill patients I saw fostered simple people. Initially, such a shallow and bigoted view made my vision too myopic to see the incredible emotional resilience and spiritual flexibility that was present and so frequently displayed around me. I was blind.

I now know that it is a vibrational thing. Quantum physics is showing us how resonance exists in all things and how everything is connected. The Force *is* with us. I know that I could feel something at times when in the presence of certain patients. At the beginning, I was numb. The sheer magnitude of the responsibilities of care, of being present, of juggling so many roles was over-whelming. I did not have the survival skills to do this even marginally well. The alpha-male in me could find no comfort in such ambiguity. Anger and defensiveness covered the fear of not knowing. Pigheaded and focused on wrong in others, I fought my way hour by hour through long days with sheer tenacity and brute logic. It was not pretty, nor was it curative. Cigarettes and exercise took an edge off; that was before alcohol found its place in my life. It did not feel good, and I would awaken on Monday mornings after a weekend off, wondering how I could survive another week of calls, emergencies, and constant

tension. On the parallel path of being in a family, I fared no better. Out of sync at all levels, I was not present at any point in my day to day. I was always in my head. Typically, I was thinking either what I needed to do, or regretting what I had done. It was a living hell.

I somehow survived in this basic combat mode till I was forty-two. Those were long years. I should have died several times. I think of the night I am driving alone in a blind drunk. I pass out going seventy miles an hour. Something unexplainable happens: I come fully awake just in time to slam on the brakes. I stumble out to see that I am less than a foot from a thirty-foot drop-off into a jagged canyon. I recall a night alone in my house, and I am drunk. I leave a large candle burning on a paper plate on my bed and pass out. I awake with a start late in the night. The candle somehow is out and not on the bed; it is on the counter. Drugs and alcohol I had around me have disappeared. Sober as I can be, I search the house and never find a trace of them. Odd.

Returning home after a long stay in treatment, I was awake to the possibility that there were Forces unseen that were seemingly at play in my life and in lives of others. This was not something primarily religious in nature; it was more complex. It was based on something in the realm of spirit. The two are not the same; my patients showed me that. They gave me the primer to a language of the heart in which so many were fluent, and that I had ignored for years.

I learn that appearances are not what they seem. So many things come to mind now. It is a Sunday when Domingo passes away in a lonely room in the hospital. In his early seventies, by the end, he'd had lost all four limbs. His penis is gone as well. I think about the cruelty of that and the suffering that it constellated. There was some irony in the sadness. While he had one arm, he was able to live in a run-down nursing home that fed him occasionally. His family had deserted him. But he seemed to smile through all of it, until one fatal day as he rides home on the bus, the driver fails to secure his wheelchair. The vehicle stops, the inertia pulls him from the back of the bus to the front. He crashes into the windshield, breaking his only arm. Then, gangrene sets in and amputation follows. No arms, no penis, no family. He does the best he can and never complains.

I am on the service the day that he dies. I see him early in the morning. He is tired, and there is a look of deep sadness that is not characteristic. I ask him if he wants anything special. He says: "Doc, I'd die for a beer." He even chuckles at his little joke. Imagine, humor in the face of such gravity. I saw it! He laughed at the complete absurdity of all of this. As I make my rounds, I think about the courage to face such darkness armed only with humility and humor.

I call the hospital kitchen. In those days, they have beer and wine for the affluent patients who come to the V.I.P. rooms on the seventh floor. It is a Sunday, and all they can

find is a can of Shaffer's. Later in the day, I go down to get the beer. Shit! They have not put it in the refrigerator. I take the warm beer to Domingo's room. He just shrugs and says, "Could you get me a straw?" He is appreciative of the gesture, and I am in awe. He spends the last hours on this earth sipping a warm Shaffer's that I hold and he drinks with a straw. He somehow finds the capacity for gratitude. This is beyond comprehension, but, I saw it.

Brenda has hepatitis C and is HIV positive. She has thick, scaly skin that weeps and bleeds where she constantly scratches. Her pruritus is unstoppable. One day, in a matter of fact way, she confides to me that she never has any relief. She itches morning and night. Before my own alcohol rehab treatment, I would have thought this was simply a symptom of dementia, but later I know better. Brenda had a level of acceptance that allowed for the unfairness inherent in her world. She was not a martyr, but a volunteer. She laughed and smiled most days I saw her and never let anyone know how much she suffered. She, like Domingo, taught me the first rules of the realm: let go of any expectation of outcome, and pray constantly for acceptance.

I was there the night she died in the hospital. I admitted her from the Emergency Room and put her in the Intensive Care Unit because her blood pressure was low. I think initially that it is a temporary thing related to her dialysis treatment that afternoon. However, as I chat with another physician while making rounds, I see her eyes

glaze over, and she vomits a yellow-green liquid. She then becomes lethargic. I know instantly that she is dying. I still feel sad that I did not see how ill she was. But, as I hold her hand and watch her leave the world, I am glad that her frail body and excoriated skin cannot drive her crazy. She will no longer have to make pretenses. In the end, she did what she knew how to do: she let go and never complained. Not once.

There was another woman, Rose, whom I took care of for years. She had no visible family support. This was so unusual in the Hispanic community. But, three times a week, she would get dropped off for dialysis by a neighbor, or someone from the church. The social worker's cash fund usually paid for her cab ride home. Paradoxically, she had the most glorious smile. She always hugged me. You could not kill her spirit.

Several years after starting dialysis, she finds out she has breast cancer. She loses both breasts and suffers alone through chemotherapy. Someone gives her a cheap wig, and she wears it like a crown. She puts on her makeup and nothing but loving words come out of her mouth. One day, I tell her that a family member has gone through the same ordeal. From that point on, she always asks about their health. She insists on hugging me and making sure that I "take care of the family." This ability to think of others was such a common trait among these mentors. They show me time and again that despite the appearance of dire circumstances, this is the best of ways to live a full life.

There are many others. Charles recently died. But, before he passed, he holds the Guinness World Record for continuous time on hemodialysis. Forty-one years! Three days a week, four hours per treatment, that is over twenty-five thousand hours sitting in a lumpy chair with large bore needles stuck into the forearm. Like so many others, he works, raises a family, and has outside interests. He is an avid motorcycle rider and completely unstoppable in his optimism.

I know another woman on the machine for twenty-five years. She does dialysis the last shift of the day because she works full time flipping hamburgers. She is a single mom and raises two stellar children. She never fails to smile and to ask about my life. That's just the type of person she is. Both of these saintly people never seem tethered to the dire drama that ravages the body. Amazingly, they are grateful for so much. They are all prone to say how thankful they are for the smallest thing. Their spirits soar even if the physical is brutal. Especially if it is brutal. They live by a mantra one once voiced: "Attitude is altitude!"

So, the basics of this life-changing dynamic were initially elusive but real. The subtle key: simply knowing that there *is* some dynamic that is larger, that involves others, that one cannot control, but can be a part of. The first imperative? Let go. Each of these people faced the most horrible things. Some, like Rose and Domingo, had no visible support. Family had abandoned them. They never had a family meal and never celebrated a

birthday among kin. They had no one to turn to in the darkness to help alleviate the inevitable pain, nausea, and suffering most all of my patients had. No one was there to scratch their back. Even the ones who had family support, like Charles, had to face alone the repeated rigors of dialysis. Yet, none of them ever gave up. Each day they simply let go of expectations, then they did their best with what they were given. There was a faith in something unseen and courage that was sustaining. Second, each of these people had an aura that one could feel. Call it what you will, they had a spirit that was palpable. It was not the product of resources, nor luck, nor anything obvious. It was something that they carried unseen. But, they knew that they had it. It was as if they were given some insular protection, based on a simple faith, which allowed them to weather the horrors that they faced on a regular basis. And when the times came that they were nearly overwhelmed, they each saw it as another degree of difficulty that they could and would accommodate. Finally, they were selfless. So many of them did not think primarily of themselves. It was so amazing to receive such blessings when someone in my family was ill or when there was a death. It was a genuine interest. The well wishes and offered prayer support were so very, very authentic. It was a natural thing that could not be feigned.

So, I remember today what my mentors have shown me: suit up, show up, and let go of expectations. They

are here watching me, I can feel them. And, I have great gratitude. They taught me that as well.

"Lude me out!"

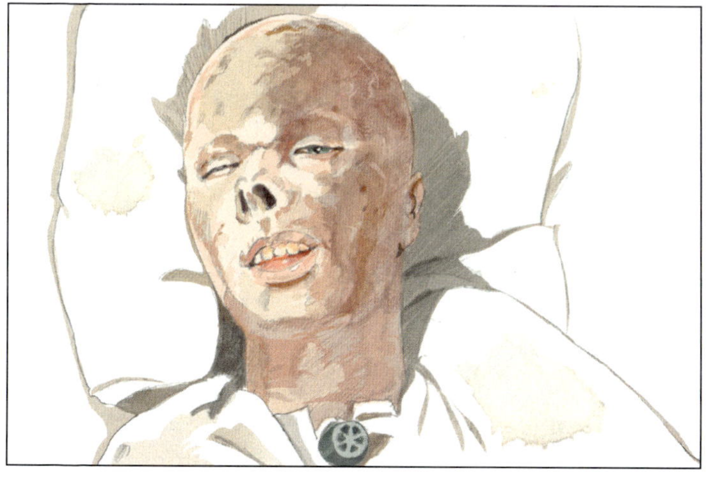

"Your real battle is not with the outside world, it is with an enemy that hides deep within you. Find it, fight it, and set yourself free. The key to your freedom lies in your deepest fear."

—HENNA SOHAIL

Much of my life, I am stubborn and learn things only in retrospect. It takes much time to decipher some of the issues. Some will never be resolved. Others are not meant to be understood. Feb-

ruary 2003, I write in my journal: "I have many voices; all of them are mine. I must own each of these. And, I must continue to try and integrate these many aspects of myself. It is awkward, and I am awkward at times. But, maybe, I am a little more fluid, a little less foolish than when I started…maybe not."

On a whim, I drive to Galveston. My first time there in thirty-four years. It is where I went to medical school. I drive down the long, ancient seawall that parallels the frothy tide. There, just beyond 81st Street, I see my old second-floor apartment at "The Seasons". I pull over and park. I look for the longest time at the balcony. Tears well up from a deep place. How odd that it still stands there. I swear, I think that I might see two young people step outside just for a moment. Perhaps he will smoke a cigarette, or the two of them will have a glass of wine. Perhaps they will hold hands and just listen to the ocean. But, the sliding glass door stays closed, much like the two years I live there. I labor over neuroanatomy and burn therapy in children. I smoke a pack of Marlboro Reds a day, drink quarts of coffee, and worry a lot. The day after graduation, with everything packed into the car, I head over the massive bridge that connects the island to the mainland. Just as I crest the high point of the causeway, the cat shits in the back seat. I take it as a sign from God. In all those years I never return. Until today.

I now clearly remember that time. It is dark and bleak. I never see the ocean calm, it is always frothy and muddy;

in constant chaos. It booms night and day. Always, it is restless and shifting. These are not comfortable days for me. So much ambiguity, so many new things. I have felt certain that medicine is the thing I should do. But, is that really just a way to please my mother? She had been a registered nurse at one point in life. She suggests medical school to me one day just after I leave the military. Who knows why she brings it up? Parents do at times try and live their unfulfilled dreams through their children. But, this was so random, and so out of her normally practical counsel. I have just completed five years as a paratrooper after graduation from West Point. I know there are worse reasons to do good things than to please one's mother. But, whatever the motive, perhaps she has a clearer vision of what life wants from me. I don't know; it does not really bother me now. However, I get there, I persist. That makes her proud in a profound way. I see it on her face. She has done her part, and I mine. But it does not make the days easy, and I am as restless the day they name me "doctor" as the previous hundreds of days and nights I spend in preparation.

The Galveston years are a meat grinder for me. The city sits on the coast of Texas. Water is an archetypal force that is in many traditions symbolic of emotion, feelings, motherhood, and the deep feminine. I see now how linear my thinking was then. How hampered I was in my ability to navigate a realm not only of the mental, but emotional, and spiritual, as well. I find an entry in my journal from

November 1998. It accurately describes my skill set at the time: "I left West Point with a very rigid and linear worldview. It was not what I was taught there, but it was my own self-constructed, self-absorptive, utilitarian approach to existence. It allowed little in the way of intuition, emotion, and introspection; but, it did provide a way to navigate in a masculine world." Perhaps, all of the unsettling I feel those long years stems from my deep feminine banished to a dark dungeon relentlessly banging on the door. Desperate to be free. Perhaps.

The training of a doctor is a curious thing. It is a gut-wrenching education in all things human and inhuman. I overhear a professor tell an associate something the day we start that long-four year trek. We are all crowded into the high tiered anatomy hall. Seated just in front of me, he leans over and says to a colleague, "My God, they all look so innocent." That man knew that so many parts of us were about to be sacrificed. He said as much when he announced to the class in his opening remarks: "One in seven of you will become an alcoholic or commit suicide, or both." The throbbing and dirty ocean is always a backdrop to the haunting things we see and learn there.

As a junior, I have a pediatric elective in the Shriners Burn Institute. There are scores of young victims who have been horribly mangled by burns of all types and causes. They are shipped in from all over the world; it is known as the best place of its kind. I remember a young teenage boy who has third-degree burns over most of his body. His

face has been horribly mangled. Scar tissue has quickly formed over his nostrils, mouth, and eyes. He has small surgical incisions made to open the orifices enough to breathe and to allow him to mumble. Many days during the three-month rotation, I hear his voice. He tries to scream, but what comes out is just a high-pitched screech. I have heard such a sound once before. A wounded, small animal screaming into the quiet night of the prairie flats near my home. The horrible shriek is alien in its intensity and pitch. One can hear it for miles. This teenage voice is just the same.

"Lude me out! Lude me out! Lude me out!" he screams. It is a chilling mantra. It is a referral to the strong tranquilizer, Quaalude. He wants desperately to be heavily sedated before they scrape off the large swaths of bacon-like textured scabs. These have to be constantly removed so that new skin can form from the base of the wounds. The gloved technicians roll him in on the gurney, then strip away his gown. Under the merciless lights, they transfer him to an aluminum lined tank. They scrub off the newly formed scabs, then hose the bleeding tissue with salt water to reduce infection. I grit my teeth and do what I am told. But I remember the screams now, and the murky water in Galveston.

Years later, before I go to treatment for alcohol abuse in Atlanta, I drink Scotch with just a little Perrier in a large Styrofoam cup most nights. I understand the desire to be heavily medicated and to simply forget some of the things

I have seen, done, and other things I have ignored. Now, separated from family, I feel as if this whole transgender transition is the equivalent of emotional burn therapy. It is odd how the whole journey loops back to teach me a form of muted compassion.

So much of my life I have been looking toward the future to provide me some relief. Or, stuck in constant review of notes from the past seeking some hidden answer. I am rarely present to see my family as they fight along-side me, nor my patients as they try to simply survive. I have rarely been emotionally available. That muting of the feminine traits of feeling, intuition, sensitivity, and compassion, seems a casualty of my medical training. Maybe in becoming a woman, I am closer to reclaiming the aspects of me that were orphaned. Those are my best parts.

I hope that I have the courage and tenacity to just survive like I saw other humans do. I hope that I have the resilience to come out on the other side with all of my faculties; scarred, but alive, and fully present. Masculine and feminine alike. In the meantime, I am a coward at times and would do a lot to just be put sleep somedays. "Lude me out, man, Lude me out." I now understand.

Tina's Story: A Tragedy

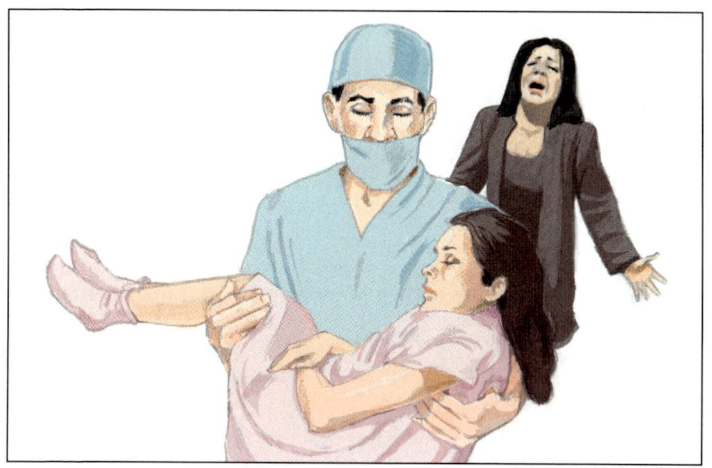

"There isn't a way things should be. There's just what happens, and what we do."

—TERRY PRATCHETT

Tina died as a teenager. I was there for all of it. I wrestle still with the memory of her precious life and her tragic death.

It is early on a brilliant spring morning. I am in my first year of a nephrology fellowship where I spend most of my time taking care of kidney transplant patients who have received organs. Part of my job is to argue with the transplant surgeon, Dr. Z., about post-operative care. In this setting, he is the absolute king. He selects the patients, harvests organs, and performs the magic of transplantation. A rotund, young faced, Caucasian from the north, he has rock star length hair, and a goatee. He is arrogant, but there is a kind edge to him. It is as if I can see through the bravado to a place deep in the heart where there is a profound caring. In retrospect, he mirrors me exactly.

He carries a phone the size and weight of a large brick. This is the way he gets immediate notification of any change in patient status, new admissions, or availability of a potential organ. From the outside, it appears that he views himself as the overlord of all aspects of the lives of his transplant patients. This is not an uncommon stance among doctors in general and surgeons in specific. However, as a fellow still in training, I do not know until I am in the midst of a year working under him, that there is an inherent conflict between transplant surgeons and nephrologists. It is a tribal gestalt: the surgeons, who do the heavy lifting and actually perform the surgery, take affront to the constant meddling from the intellectually oriented nephrologists. There are daily arguments over medications, fluid status, diet, and immunosuppression schedules. "But, Dr. Z., I think we need to taper her pred-

nisone more quickly. The side effects are just devastating,"
I say. "It is a protocol that I've used for years, and it has
worked well. Show me evidence in the literature that it
should not be applied here, and we'll talk," he says. "Otherwise, do what I say." It is not a blood feud, but there is
real passion in the arguments. These decisions can and
do mean life or death.

Tina is born with diabetes and high blood pressure. Her
diet is as unhelpful as is the heavy albatross of her gene
pool. My experiences to this point in medicine show me
one thing: chronic disease is a trail of tears. It is especially
caustic when it arrives early in a life. No disease bears this
out like kidney failure. Tina is no exception. The weight of
a random universe seemingly crashes down on her young
body, and the carnage is insidious. Hormonal patterns rage,
blood pressure anomalies explode, bones weaken, organs
falter and fail. With no recourse, dialysis is necessitated
in the emotional quagmire that marks her teenage years.

The initiation is vulgar. It begins with vascular surgery
in the arm. A vein is married with a small artery. Large
serpiginous venous channels arise. The arm swells and
the vein looks like a small rope under thin skin. It cannot
be hidden. However, it serves a purpose: nurses cannulate these thickened veins with needles the size of bobby
pins. This is how the blood gets out of the body and to the
machine. For four infinite hours three days a week, Tina
sits in a cheap recliner. Her schooling is an after-thought.
She will never worry about a prom dress.

Like her often crippled adult companions, she learns to adapt. She is a survivor. She is at once a needy and loving mascot for all who take care of her. She smiles, yet there are days when she is shaken and in pain. It is not fair, and we all know that. She is the youngest dialysis patient I know. At an age when she should have been going to the mall with her friends or learning geometry, she is drafted into a life of doctors, nurses, needles, blood, and pain. The stormy realm of end-stage renal disease is difficult for the strongest of adults to negotiate. For Tina, it is absolute Purgatory. Besides the strict diet, the multiple medications, the marathon dialysis treatments, there is the drama of early puberty. Body image is a battleground in the best of teen life settings, but with rapid weight gains, the bizarre anatomic distortion inherent with access surgery, and constant fatigue, pimples are only a small part of the horror-filled litany that is her journey. Tina does the best she can.

She has a proud, strong-willed, supportive mother. Young and pretty with Castilian features, she has been abandoned by her husband. Left to float in a land where she does not speak the language, she is clever in a well-intentioned way. She lives in constant fear. It is a fear of loss, of not having enough, of not being enough. Having a child who needs access to the monolithic institution of healthcare is a nightmare. But, Tina's mother uses her fear as a fulcrum. She is relentless. She demands care for her daughter, asks tough questions of the nurses, and

confronts the arrogance of doctors. She is the priestess of a large clan working night and day cleaning houses to support everyone. Tina is one among many. The other children have many needs as well. But, the mother gives what she can and loves her girl the best she knows how.

Tina and her mother eye me for a long time, not knowing what to make of a doctor in training. But, in the end, I am trusted.

If I had been honest and could have seen everything objectively, from the very start I knew that the odds were terribly small that this would turn out well. I think Tina's mother knew that in her heart. She was the most honest among us. But, altruism is a salve I use to cover the emotional wounds that are inevitable when taking care of people this ill. I get close, and their loss cuts deeps. Blindly lurching forward without emotional involvement is a technique in this dark realm, but I have not yet learned how to do that.

I quickly learn a few basics about providing care in this setting: first, movement is a positive. Sit still, and you have time to think. Second, the first casualty of dialysis in the young is hope. The blood, pain, boredom, and trauma of life on a machine drain long-term visions. The anticipation for a future that supports lovely dreams in a younger Tina is easily crushed. She learns to just get through today. Smile, play the role, get off dialysis, go home, sleep. Repeat.

It is in the midst of this cauldron of darkening flux

that a seeming miracle occurs. Think of the euphoria that Tina feels when she is called to get a kidney transplant. No more dialysis, no more needles, no more hiding her arms. She can date, she can drink a Coke, she can live her life. The surgeon offers this hope.

She and the mother hear all of the potential negatives while signing the release for surgery. Of course, they don't believe anything but good will occur from this point on. Surgery is performed. But, post operatively, all hell breaks loose. Each of the horrors that can complicate an organ transplant manifest in their worst forms. Tina's body does not embrace the new kidney and there is acute rejection. The surgeon and I argue about doing dialysis, which I think she needs. He is of the mindset that doing dialysis at this early point damages the psyche and reduces the chances that the organ does well over time. We finally do dialysis; Tina is crushed. But, somehow, she responds to this and to large doses of anti-rejection medication. Despite the side effect of massive weight gains from fluid retention caused by the medicine and a barely functional kidney, there is some response. Urine is being made! The lab work begins to improve. She has a day, then two, where she can eat and walk! There is joy.

I remember the day that Tina leaves the hospital. She, her mother, and the clan are treated like royalty. There are balloons, a cake, cards, and well-wishes from the nursing staff, lab personnel, and the janitors. Everyone come to say goodbye! It is such a good day. We all feel

that we have been a part of something good and clean. There is a collective and palpable warmth that unites us as we stand in this moment.

If the story ended with the discharge, I would not remember it this many years later. But, over the next six months, there are complications. Tina's return to the hospital Emergency Room in the middle of the night becomes common. The E.R. doctor says to me time and again when he calls, "Tina is in; she doesn't look good." First, it is a fever, then decreasing urine, then skin pustules, then a productive cough. Each presentation demands a long stay. Tina becomes what the E.R. nurses call, "a tar-baby". She is tethered to the hospital and cannot escape. She, her mother, the doctors, and nurses, are all married and mired in a horrific dance.

I can see Tina, horribly bloated, barely recognizable, moaning. The mother sobbing. The team marches in, then the surgeon looks at the numbers on the chart. I offer, "I think she needs dialysis." He says, "We'll wait. This looks better." We walk out, the mother is screaming, "Fix my child, fix my child." We do dialysis when things get to the point where Tina cannot breathe. This gets to be a regular pattern. The stays in the hospital are usually one or two weeks. There is enough return of kidney function to let her go home, but these are not joyful discharges. They become brief respites where she and the staff can gather themselves for the intense and horror-filled days that are looming. Always looming.

There is one thing that remains paramount in all of this: maintenance of the vein that is the means to receive dialysis. The large bore access that she has in her left arm is a lifeline. It is the one way that we can insert dialysis needles to remove the waste and fluids that she cannot clear with her own, marginal kidney function. With no access, urgent dialysis is dependent on insertion of a large catheter in a subclavian or femoral vein. But, Tina's large veins have been sacrificed in repeated use for I.V. therapy. She is unprotected.

Just before her last discharge, Tina's access clots. It will not work. There is no way to do dialysis. There are simply no good choices. Surgery to create another access is impossible as she has no more veins. Ultimately, discharge means that unless there is a miracle, she will return sooner than later with no ability to clear fluid or toxic wastes from the body. She is doomed either way.

That final morning, Tina cannot breathe. She is full of fluid and potassium. It is a lethal combination. From their home, the hysterical mother calls, then drives to the hospital with Tina in the back seat. The surgeon meets them at the front door. A convoy of nurses and screaming support staff trail him as he rushes down the hall with Tina in his arms. She is in full arrest. We find a room and start CPR. We intubate her, shock her, try to find a vein to give medications. By the end, she has needle pricks all over her precious body. Of course, there are no veins. Tina dies in front of me.

Years before, I see the Pietà in a museum in Europe. It is magical to see what has been captured in stone. There is a loving, overwhelming angst that is present around this famous statue. Words and pictures don't convey the compassion that is touchable in its presence. In holding the body of her son Jesus, the infinite sadness and sense of loss of Mary are truly palpable. It is a sacred space.

Now years later, I think of the surgeon and how he held Tina's body that last day as he rushed down the hall. It so reminds me of the Pietà. That doctor loved her, and he did all he knew how to do to give her a life. We all did. It was simply not enough.

I know now that no one was at fault. People just do the best they can, and terribly dark things happen in this world. As a transgender woman, I am beginning to understand this reality. There are times these crazy days in my own transition that I think about all of this. I think about what Tina's mother must have felt after it was all over, after the funeral and drama. I am sure that it must have seemed that she was mother of a child relegated to a denizen of a lesser god.

I know this: these were heroic and complex people. How noble to live confronting such darkness against over-whelming odds. Each morning Tina and her mother got up, both likely sensing, in some inexplicable way, that all of this was far-fetched, that doom loomed like a large cloud on the horizon. They knew that despite the love, the doctors, the medicine, the transplant, the chances were

slim that things would turn out well. But, this was the most remarkable fact: they did their best at every point with what they were given.

Today, I feel the hope, I feel the despair, I feel the pain, and I keep going. I have been shown by a group of remarkable teachers that there is a way to effectively maneuver in this darkness. I will do *my* best. Tina and her mother demand nothing less.

Requiem: Paw-Paw

"Miracles happen every day. Not just in remote country villages or at holy sites halfway across the globe, but here, in our own lives."

—DEEPAK CHOPRA

I know this: there are great mysteries that surround us. I spent many years asleep to the ebb and flow of larger Forces that work in ways I cannot fathom. It is the greatest of gifts to have had my eyes opened in later years to the reality of such process. Such great teachers have appeared! Now, awake to the improbable made manifest, I cannot readily explain many things that I have experienced. They are beyond words. My gratitude becomes the only adequate response.

I knew Dora before becoming her physician. Early in my practice years, her daughter was a patient. Fathered by one of several husbands, the daughter is a sweet and

gentle soul. Sadly, she is horribly afflicted with ravaging diabetes mellitus and high blood pressure. In her late teens, overweight to an extreme, she spirals into kidney failure.

Diabetics with end-stage renal disease have a heartbreaking path. Elevated blood pressure combines with uncontrolled blood sugar levels to wreck vessel integrity. These forces relentlessly destroy small blood vessels feeding all parts of the body. Compromised blood flow suffocates function. Limbs and organs are serially destroyed. Legs. Arms. Eyes. Heart. The sad paradox: a longer life from dialysis treatments prolongs a journey full of heartbreak. Most days on dialysis rounds, I count two score limbs missing from my small flock. Leg prostheses, temporarily removed for comfort, lay by patient dialysis chairs like props in a bad dream. Many have multiple limbs missing. This brutal drama of limb and organ loss plays out over long periods of time. Usually years. Even with gangrene, feet rot slowly. Day after day, pain and disability hover. The grieving for the loss of one's own body is a constant struggle. This cannot be rushed nor ignored. Month after month, these souls must bear witness to their own slow death.

Dialysis is an unforgiving gauntlet. Three days a week, two large bore needles the size of small and slender nails are cannulated deep into swollen arms. Blood circulates from one needle, through the dialysis filter, then is pumped back into the body via a second needle. It takes four hours to cleanse the waste and remove the volume

that the failed kidneys cannot handle. Life reduces to these essentials: a bland diet with little meat, no salt, no dairy, and two glasses of water a day. Taste evaporates, libido fails; and, in many, especially in diabetics, small strokes lessen cognition. Fluid is restricted because scant urine is made. There is chronic thirst. Skin becomes leathery and dry. Even worse, neither the body nor the dialysis filter can clear dietary phosphorus, found especially in milk products. The mineral, so vital to life, becomes an irritant to the already dehydrated skin. Night and day the itching curses many. Always thirsty, tied to a machine, limbs whittled off, sight lost, mental skills reduced, florid itching constant, it is a true hell. Only the most tenacious survive. Most everyone is gone within five years. Death is the only constant.

Early on, Dora's daughter does fairly well. She receives a transplant, and things level out for several years. However, her body slowly rejects the organ. In the end, she is forced to return to dialysis. To make things worse, she retains the puffy, bloated face caused by the anti-rejection medicines that have failed her. It is during this time that her mother comes to see me in the clinic about her own health issues. In earlier days, Dora is strikingly pretty and takes good care of herself. That slowly changes. The day I tell her that she needs dialysis, she breaks down and sobs like a child. I do too.

The first several years Dora and her daughter manage as best they can. There are no major issues. Life becomes

at least tolerable. Because of finances and family, they move to a smaller town. However, I happen to oversee dialysis there as well, where it is performed in cramped space at the local hospital. At the most, the procedure area is fifteen feet by twenty feet. By necessity, recliners and dialysis machines are bunched tightly. Eight patients per shift, the lack of privacy and close quarters make it especially difficult for all. Yet, like guardian angels, there are dedicated nurses to tend to these desperate patients. Everyone does the best they can.

Given the limited dialysis area, I am always concerned with the possibility of a patient passing out and the nurses calling a "code". Obviously, resuscitation in such a setting is horribly difficult. Over the years, there is only a very occasional "code blue". If I, or a partner is not there, a physician rushes up from the E.R. as the nurses begin resuscitation. If the defibrillator is used to electrically restart the heart, it is macabre. The helpless body of a patient flops with every shock. Nurses and doctors screaming orders and answers. The other dialysis patients are unfortunate bystanders. Hooked, literally, to their machines, they are forced to look on. There is no escape.

Imagine sitting in a chair on dialysis with your only daughter just across the room. How would it feel to see her suddenly pass out? Immediately, the nurses start life support. Dora is hysterical. The trauma of the code crescendos. The daughter does not respond. With the paddles administering shock after shock, the lifeless body

flops and jerks. There is vomiting, blood, and chaos. Her precious daughter dies in a heap of paper and screaming nurses. One cannot paint a clearer picture of hell.

Dora was never the same. How could she be? She bravely struggles on. But, from that point on, her eyes bear such heavy sadness. Then, the worst possible thing happens: Dora passes out one day. It is a massive stroke. I never understand how she survives. But, she does.

During my practice years, I rotate into the hospital one week out of every three. I am the one to admit her, and at the end of the week I sadly think that I have seen her for the last time. To my surprise, on my next rotation, I stop by the rehabilitation area to see another patient and there Dora is! She is propped in a wheelchair; hair clean, makeup carefully applied by some loving soul. She smiles a smile that I cannot forget. The stroke has claimed half of her. Nothing works on the right face and left body. She has a beautiful, mischievous-looking, crooked smile. When she talks, all that comes out is a single sound: "paw". When she tries to converse, it is a sing-song of "paw-paw-paw-paw". There are inflections, but using the same, repeated, guttural sound.

I visit her over the next few months. She always seems glad to see me. I feel the same. Linked in some mysterious way during that time, the most radical thing occurs. As Dora tries to talk, the intonation and rhythm become more sophisticated. It is like someone practicing daily to learn Morse Code. It is always the same word, but repeatedly

used, it sounds like an alien language. There is one other remarkable thing: I understand everything she is trying to say. I know what she wants to tell me.

This unnerves me in lots of ways. Perhaps it would not have done so had it happened before I went to treatment for alcoholism. But, after that time, I am more sensitive. The first years in practice, I remember being an arrogant prick. But, in the six months of 1993 that I mop floors in a mission in downtown Atlanta, I learn some humility. Something settles deep within me during that time. I change in-spite of great inner resistance.

In retrospect, I view this strange fluency with Dora as a gift of that sobriety. I am dumbfounded. But, I am grateful. She lovingly becomes, "Paw-Paw" to me. It is a term of endearment. The language and my understanding of it bonds us spiritually in a very concrete way. It is a remarkable gift that we share. She is no longer locked into an interior world. Someone understands. For me, it is as if I have been given some reward for continuing my sober journey.

Over time, she tells me many things. She recounts how horrible it is to see her daughter die in front of her. We talk about her depression, about her fear of death, about her feelings of insignificance. Verbalizing those things helps relieve some great inner tension. I do understand this: it is a terrible thing to be dependent, discounted, and irrelevant. The fear that explodes in that construct is devastating to mind, body, and spirit. But, Dora talks and I listen. Her fluency heals us both.

I am on call the morning Paw-Paw dies. They notify me at home. She has become unresponsive. I rush to the Medical Intensive Care Unit. She is not there. They call and say they are still coding her. I cannot bring myself to go to her part of the hospital. I can't bear to watch that traumatic ritual of resuscitation: the intubation, chest compressions, and repeated electrical shocks. I silently pray that she dies without suffering. But, after forty-five minutes of compressions, numerous rounds of strong stimulants, and repeated shocks, her heart somehow begins to beat again. There is a rhythm, then her blood pressure returns. It is then that they wheel her to the Unit.

The code team moves her from the stretcher. Celia, the wise old crone of a charge nurse, accepts care as they deposit her body in a bed on the left, down near the exit. She tries to clean her up. I seek to do an assessment. The intubation tube has been removed as she is somehow breathing on her own. She gasps deeply, and moves her mouth. We both stop: she is making some sort of incredible recovery! But, her mouth closes tightly and she begins to purse her lips. Called a "fish mouth", it is never a good thing. Celia and I look at each other; she says in a soft voice, "Doctor, she's dying." I know that. At that moment, I hate it worse than anything I could ever imagine. Dora and I are bound by some unexplainable miracle. The prospect of losing a link to that deeper Mystery creates a deep, deep void in me. We do what we can, Celia holds one hand and I the other. Dora opens her eyes once and

I know she recognizes me. She nods. Then she whispers: "Paw-Paw." Then she is gone.

In the years since, I think often of this unlikely story. I remember my friend. And, when I think about an afterlife, I hope only this: that in that perfect world there is justice. I hope those that are innocent and who live with unspeakable things happening to them, like Dora, move with death into some special realm. I pray it is some mystical, magical Nirvana where all good things come to pass, all day, every day. Special dispensation. For all the innocents who suffer so very much while alive, I hope there is great comfort in passing. For those who have stared into the abyss and have not flinched, there *should* be some special reward. I hope that's true. I hope my great teacher Paw-Paw is there with her daughter. Both of them young, beautiful, laughing, talking. Smiling.

Me, I am honored to have known such good people. It is what I do. I sense that I am a guardian who helps others over thresholds, over the Abyss. I feel this strongly in the gender clinic that I attend in each week. Marginalized, with a suicide rate of over forty percent, transgender people are attacked by bigoted politicians and insensitive followers in the same way that blacks, gays, and women have been savaged in the past. Such lovely people, such great courage they teach me. They are my heroes. I mean that with the deepest reverence. Best of all, they continue to take care of my heart in special ways. As a result, I am being healed in some deep, meaningful way.

To one special woman, I owe a great debt. She once taught me a whole new language that I could never have known. And when it's my time, I hope Paw-Paw comes to find me and leads me home.

Wagagai

"Pilgrimage to the place of the wise is to find escape from the flame of separateness."

—RUMI

It is an early African morning, 3 February 2009. I am in the depths of eastern Uganda with ten others from the flatlands of West Texas. We are doing medical mission work. Our surgeon leader has guided volunteers here for years. This is my second trip. The first, I came because of the novelty. I return having been struck deeply by the spirit of the land and people. There is also a shared, simple intimacy with the team: it translates to a palpable compassion.

People we tend to are ill. When I see them, I give needed medication and heart-felt guidance. No lengthy electronic medical record keeping, no insurance to file, no Medicare. There are simply sick people and a doctor. I sit and listen to each tell a story, then do my best to help. In that exchange, there is something palpable and profoundly good.

On clinic days, we arrive at one of the mud brick churches that dot the hinterland. They are the hubs of an extended community life. Typically, there are no glass windows and no electricity. The floors, though, are smooth from constant sweeping, and the low benches clean. These spaces are lovingly tended. By 8:00 am there are hundreds of fresh-scrubbed men, women, shy children, and stooped-back elders reverently standing in a long line. These are elegant people. The women in bright, brilliantly colored, and sparkling, kimono-type dresses. Men in clean, if thread-bare, suits with smooth, shaved Nubian faces. All are here to see *us*.

Anticipation is electric as the day starts. There is a ritual that my interpreter and I develop. He leads the patients in and points to a bare bench. I then stand and shake an outstretched hand. We will do this scores of times. Sitting in front of me is a mother with luminous, dark brown eyes. She holds a young boy to her breast. His head is not right, it is too large, and does not seemingly fit the bony body. This is Kwashiorkor. It is what protein malnourishment looks like. My diagnosis helps little; we are years too late. I simply reassure the mother to continue with her loving care. A young man plops down. He is malnourished, gaunt, and does not look me in the eye. He is only one of a handful of single men. There are dime-sized lesions and scabs on his face. He has fever, and teeth that are going bad. It takes little history to realize: this is untreated AIDS. I encourage him to go to a clinic

in Kampala. He leaves, disgusted by my lack of resources. I cannot forget the face and the shame I feel at not being able to help. What am I doing here? Inadequacy sits deep in my stomach, and no matter the hugs or heartfelt appreciation of many, I leave each day, thinking one thing: I should have given more. Years later, I still struggle with the conundrum.

There is something else transformative about this trip to a country, now deep in my bones. I am climbing, with a guide, the huge peak just east of Mbale. Mount Elgon is one of the ten tallest in Africa. It is actually a ring of ancient volcanic peaks, a "caldera". Wagagai, my destination, looms above the rest. The name translates roughly to "where God is".

I catch myself smiling in the mirror of the room at the Mount Elgon Hotel the day of my departure. I think, "This is a Forrest Gump type of day." It's years before my transgender issues will fully manifest, but for some reason I feel so powerfully feminine, like a warrior princess. It is odd.

My life is littered with such odd initiations and unanticipated thresholds. I am the Fool-Child once again. Am I prepared for the unfolding that lies just ahead? The adventure begins as Rose picks me up in her small, black Hyundai. She is in her mid-thirties. A smooth, kind, face, and deep, flat cornrow braids in shining black hair. I cannot get past a sense of sadness that lingers just beyond our greeting. Later, as we twist and turn up a dirt road leading into the mountains east of Mbale, she does the

queerest thing. She turns, looks at me, and pulls off a wig. She is nearly bald. She laughs, then stuffs the hair piece in a small bag, and ties a vanilla colored scarf tight on her head. We are headed to the bar and small hotel she owns. In some mystical way, I feel that we are kindred spirits.

As we travel, she tells me her story. Oldest of four girls in a large Ubishu family, a marriage is arranged at an early age. She fights violently with her father but has no recourse. Several years into an abusive relationship, she has a horrible car accident. Her young child dies instantly. She is taken to a local hospital and given up for dead. Despite broken bones and heart, she survives. After a year of recuperation, she emerges reborn. She divorces her husband, and leaves her village. She buys, on credit, the land on the side of the mountain road where she had the wreck. It is the home of her new life. From those ashes, she builds a thriving business on her own terms. The name of the compound? "Rose's Last Chance."

I depart from her homestead the next morning with a rucksack full of canned beans and energy bars. Moses, my guide, looks at me in a quizzical way. I know, by his looks, that he is fully aware that there is a dangerous threshold ahead and, I suspect he judges I am not sufficiently ready. He is right.

The backpack weighs fifty pounds. Thirty minutes into the first part of the climb, I have sweated through my shirt. There is no flat ground. The temperature and humidity rise with each step. I have trained, but for this

journey the Stair Master at my local gym is not sufficient preparation. The slope is a monster.

Till now, in my two trips to Uganda, I have seen beauty, grace, and sensitivity. This is radically different. It is chthonic. It is me with my face being pushed into a reality. This is the darker side of a desperately tough land. Only the strong survive here. By the end of the first six hours, I am dead tired. I drink most of my water, change shirts twice, and ruin my camera with dripping sweat. I am face to face with some ancient and archetypal force. It demands the best I have. If I cannot summon it, I will not make it back. Nine hours later, and some seventeen kilometers up a thankless path, I am stopping every fifty meters to bend over. I am so desperately tired; I want only to catch my breath. We crest a hill and see a small hut in the fading light. I am in tears when Moses says, "We are here."

I sleep deeply. There are large but unremembered dreams. Somehow, with fresh water and rest, I am prepared as we launch out the next morning. We leave our heavy packs behind as we plan to be at the summit by noon and back to our base several hours later. That is the plan. There is ice on the ground, and it is bitter cold in the shallow, dawn light. The sun begins to rise and warm my steps. Late the previous day, we had climbed out of a forest of bamboo into barren terrain. Now, I can see juniper, scrub brush, and sage dotting most angles of the steep canyon walls that undulate on both sides. We are

near four thousand meters in elevation. There are multitudes of delicate, nickel-sized, white and crimson flowers painting color-filled seas around the rocks and grist. Like everything here, pretty or not, only heartiness is relevant.

My legs are sore, but I feel the call of something special at hand. Lactic acid drains as we ply upward. I see a monstrous peak looming. Moses crushes my hopes when he says, "You cannot see the one we are going to." Hours later, I am in a good rhythm. We begin to walk along a thick ridge. I look up, two peaks loom to our right. He points to the further and says, "There she is." The peak stays in my vision as we stumble up the sixty-degree slopes. We are nearing the summit.

I turn and look back to the eastern sky. The slope skirts out to fingers of smaller peaks. Below them, a heavy layer of clouds. I stand above them and peer down to the Kenyan countryside just below. I spy a small lake, perhaps fifty meters wide. It reflects the golden, late-morning light. Something in the water creates two narrow and perfectly parallel wakes. The sun makes it too bright to see if it is a pair of ducks or something beneath the surface. Incredibly, the trails are perfectly in alignment. I am reminded: there is such mystery in this alien land.

I peer for a hundred miles deep into the cavernous Rift Valley. The caldera morphs back toward the flatland. With the sun now rising further, the lands below look backlit and draped in dark blue and maroon. This is home of man; of me and mine. I am "where God is."

I cannot stop scanning the vista. We shuffle the last few steps. I kneel down and now face to the west. I am in a holy space. Nothing needs to tell me that, I know it at the core. The air is full of a shimmering. It is something subliminal and Sacred. A clear thought arises: "Leave something in homage". Of course, this a traditional part of pilgrimage that has been practiced for millennia. I wear a heart-shaped ivory pendant given to me ten years before. It has the scent of my life, my family, my patients, my mentors, my dead father. I take it off. I offer a simple prayer and toss it far down the slope. It will not likely be found by a human for many years to come.

We take the route back, gather our things, and by the end of the day drop down another two thousand meters. I am dog tired and completely spent. In the sleeping bag in my solitary tent I listen as the soft African rain pelts down. I drift into a dreamless sleep with one thought: I have been led over a great threshold.

On return home, I am asked, "What did you see?" I know now, as I only suspected then, that as I sat sponge-like, drinking in the light and the brush of winds on that Ugandan peak, Something at that moment was surveying *through* me. For a moment in time: I was the eyes, ears, tongue, and mouth of the Ineffable. On that crested berm, high over the alien spread of the most foreign of lands, I felt truly at home. Whatever held me was not passive. The Force that blew through me in that unknowable way somehow synchronized all the discord that I had come

with. That morning, I was opened in some tender and intimate way to a larger way of Being. It is something that rattles and reminds me still: I am given specific things that need my tending.

I know also, there is an inevitable price to pay for radical pilgrimage: on return, life can never be the same.

Acceptance

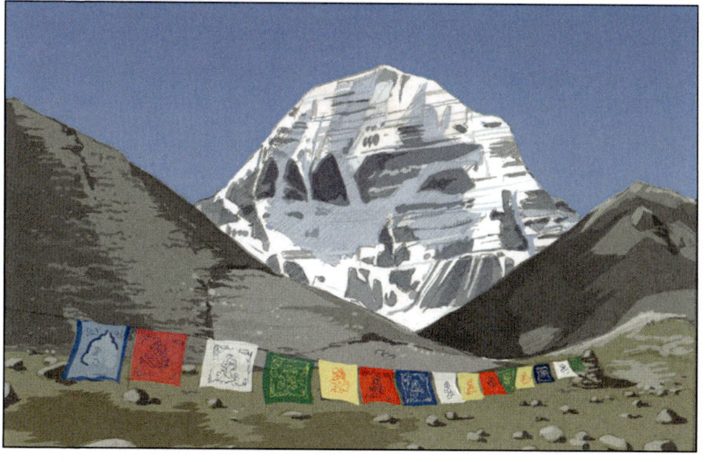

"I realize how many aspects of myself that I am unaware of. There are the needy, arrogant, dark parts that I just don't want to see, and especially, don't have any desire to own."

—JOURNAL, AUGUST 2000

I think of my time with Bret, Barry, and Tom. Three brothers who have a hereditary kidney abnormality called autosomal dominant polycystic kidney disease (ADPKD). The mother, Dorothy, a lovely woman,

is already on dialysis. I am the physician for all four. The insidious part of this malady is that it manifests primarily between the ages of thirty and forty. Just at the point where life, labor, and vigor are at their sweetest and steadiest, disaster hits. Full of relentlessly enlarging cysts, the kidneys fail. Dialysis or organ transplantation become the only options. Lives, jobs, and marriages are all radically altered in the process. Nothing is left unchanged.

In a family with ADPKD, there is no certain way to predict who will progress on to renal failure. High blood pressure is a modifier, diet and lifestyle choices can have an impact, but in the end, the odds are one in three that siblings will reach end stage. I talk with each of these men for years about who among them has "the black bean". They are all such good men, each with families that they adore. Like so many decent people I have known in medicine, they take care of the things in front of them. As the years pass, each seems accepting of whatever fate awaits. Acceptance in the face of such potential darkness speaks to great courage and strength and a faith in Something abiding.

It is early dawn in August 2011. I am on the second day of the thirty-five mile kora around Mount Kailash in western Tibet. In an hour we begin the ascent up the Dromola. It is a brutally steep mountain pass angling near sixty degrees. For centuries this is heralded as the heart of the journey. For four hours I will trudge step by difficult step upward on the narrow trail. Standing just

outside of the tent, I look up and see the radical beauty of the eastern face of that ancient mountain. It is pristine. New snow bellows high into the air and the crystals reflect an unearthly light, then a rainbow appears. Being there at that one spot in that one moment opens something deep inside. I feel re-connected to a resonance that is full of peace. At that point in time, I am not surfing into the future nor reconciling some minor aspect of "me". I am not in opposition to anything. I am just present. I am content: with me, with everything. I know then, if only for a moment, what it means to be at home in this world. Bret, Barry, and Tom all seem familiar with this terrain.

In the end, Bret draws the black bean. He may have had some premonition as before that downward spiral, he takes his family on a long vacation to Hawaii. Later, in the office, he shares with me picture after beautiful picture. I still remember the belly laughs we share. He was so proud of his family.

I move my practice before the kidney failure reaches a bottom. I am glad, in a selfish sort of way, that I did not have to see my friend go through the trauma of starting dialysis. It would have been hard seeing such an active man so full of life and vigor at an earlier point, sitting in the dialysis chair. Bret did it, and, I am certain, he did it without complaint.

I talk to him several times after I leave. He always has such a positive attitude. It is not feigned, he really feels grateful to simply be alive. He is a religious man. We

never delve deeply into his beliefs, but, I do know that he knew he felt that he was part of something larger. He felt blessed to be alive, to be human. Bret showed me this: the ability to be comfortable in one's own skin despite any and all calamity. It is what I think about now. It was not the specifics of his religion, but it was a faith that he displayed. A profound belief in some coherent whole of which he and I are both somehow a part. Sometimes, I think I understand that better now. It is always fleeting, but when I do, I feel at home. Bret taught me how to live in the world. I forget it some days, though. Those are the days that seem long and take the wind out of me.

I have been on this transgender path in earnest for four years. Like Bret's process, it is something that I have struggled with for a long time. I think of the first blush and make-up that I wore at the age of five. I can recount the intoxication I feel the first time putting on a yellow chiffon nightgown. I cannot forget the first "makeover" I have at the hands of a female makeup artist in Houston. Her business is, appropriately called, "Criss-Cross". I see now in vivid detail that April morning in 2013, when it becomes clear to me: "I am a woman." I have been on hormone replacement therapy now for three years. I have developed flattened, but rounded breasts. My eyelashes have grown noticeably, the fine lanugo hair on my chest and face is scattered. The monthly waxing is ongoing. Electrolysis is scheduled but, like the facial feminization surgery, is something around the corner. There is some lift

to the syntax of my voice as I am devoted to the practice of voice feminization. A laryngeal surgical intervention will be done at some point. This will raise my voice from the 145 MHz male to a 220 MHz female register. I will have the voice of a woman. Bottom surgery, the Holy Grail, where I finally become a woman with a vagina, is on the far horizon. But, I have had good mentors, and in my heart and soul, I am committed. That is the whole point: I have committed. The dysphoria, the sense of being ill at ease in my body, is just an aspect of an unfolding process. Bret understood this. He faced it all with grace and kindness.

These things wash over me as I read his obituary. Having received a kidney transplant several years prior, he passes unexpectedly. His journey has ended. I regret that I never took time to go to a baseball game with him and Barry. They had season tickets to the games of a local team and were as diligent about taking time to watch as they were about taking care of their business. It was the same spirit, just different venues. The construct of Bret's life was simple: always putting one foot in front of another, one just does the next right thing. That is living in the present. He was an expert.

I wonder how Bret's religious beliefs would have squared with me being transgender? My brain thinks he would strongly reject it, but my heart knows that he lived accepting all things just as they are. He faced the light and the dark within and without, and when he died, he was "at home". I think in all those times we sat in my office

that he secretly gave me a detailed map for becoming Sheila Grace. Today, just now, I accept it. It is darker and different from what I would have thought I would get, but who am I to judge? I know my friend faced his own monstrous challenges. So, I will do what he showed me to do: accept it, be grateful, help others in the process. I am certain he would approve.

Passages

"Let the world kiss you, sister. Let the moment kiss the most raw and tender spot in your heart until you cannot help but surrender, open."

—CHAMELI ARDAGH

It is 2016, and I am retired. I am driving to West Texas for a funeral. As I do, the names and faces break through the mental boundary that I have hidden so much behind. They cannot be forgotten. So many good people.

Buddy was a special man. He had been a patient for years and years. His death rattles me, and I need to be present at the funeral. I need to feel the warmth that comes from the grace that is the residue of people caring about people. I'd kept up with his wife, Sharon. Both of them were stellar nurses. They each did their nursing work like everything else: the best they could, each and every day. In this dark time, she needs support. I need to pay respects, but mostly, I need to see family. That is what this is really about.

There are 339 miles in this journey. I know every turn in the road. The mesquite dotted flats stretch north for a hundred miles. 442 times I drove that long route. Honestly, I cried every single time I drove back from a weekend at home. But, I did it because it was a calling. Certainly the money was important. But, I knew this was what I was supposed to do. Like my transgender journey, it is something that comes from the deepest part of me. I hated many things about that period in my life, but so many solid people made it all worthwhile. Buddy was one of those.

He had been on dialysis when I arrived. He worked when he could. I know now he never really felt well. Some days were better than others, but he never felt good. He never complained. Not once. He had a booming, deep Nat King Cole-like, gravel voice from the years of cigarettes. He'd laugh from his belly and break out that big, almost goofy smile whenever I'd see him on dialysis. He always asked me how I was. Always. He was genuinely interested. We'd share a joke, and that's when that smirk and laugh would come. Sharon worked on the medical floor at the hospital. She was such a strong presence. She ran a well-tended service like the professional she was. She took care of people with a passion.

Sharon cared, so did Buddy. People, especially the chronically ill and their tribe, know when you reciprocate that care. It's part of a deep emotional reflex that must come with such brutal and repeated trauma. It guides them in knowing whom to trust. They just know. With that

unspoken link, there is always a bedrock of love. These generous and courageous people will let you into their hearts. But without the knowledge that one truly cares, one can be the best doctor in the universe, and they will not let you get close.

I get to the funeral home early. It is just west of the country club, on the fringe of town. Pump-jacks sprout like alien beasts in this latest version of an oil boom. Dust is high in the air, and the wind blows as it always does. But that wind never stopped Buddy from his beloved golf. He will be laid to rest a seven-iron from the course, so I suspect it is okay by him. I wonder why I never played golf with Bud. We talked about it frequently. I was no good, but Buddy would have been glad for me to tag along. I think about that now. Regret is a heavy thing.

I see people I have not seen for years. We smile, and there are hugs. Good, deep, "I mean it" hugs. I talk with Sharon. We laugh about Buddy being too stubborn to die. That is close to the truth. I can tell that she appreciates that I know how special her husband has been. Such affirmation makes such dark passage more bearable. I had made the effort, and she knew I did it out of respect.

It is a simple service. Three-quarters of the plainly furnished chapel is full. There are three full rows of family. They have a slide show. There is Bud with a full deck of hair, and a beard too. There he is on a derrick during his roughnecking days. There he is playing golf and sitting in his easy chair. In almost all pictures there are kids. I don't

see many slides without family. How pretty Sharon was, and Bud handsome in a rough-cut way. Him in the robin's egg blue tux at the wedding. More of the grandkids. He always seems to be gently hugging one or having one in his lap in that old recliner. He looks like an old monarch. God, I hope that he felt justified in his realm. He earned such comfort. A regal spirit in a random land. I feel closer to both Buddy and Sharon seeing those special moments.

Lord knows they had a hard go with the brutal nature of dialysis. I had seen Buddy at his worst, with fever, vomiting, bleeding, and desperate illness. I did not have to see him pass from this realm. I am a little ashamed but am glad for that. My nurse practitioner, and one of the best men I have ever know, told me over coffee that he had been there for the end. Buddy had a big vegetation on one of his heart valves, and it finally started to shed. Pieces of debris swirled downstream into the small arteries that feed the brain. Bud got confused; then he went down. They intubated him, but by then he was gone. Sharon, like the angel she is, said "no more". Her best friend had done his best and suffered enough. She had enough courage to say "goodbye" and to let him go in peace.

I knew Bud near the end of that well lived life. The eight years that I was one of his doctors flew by, but I loved being his physician. He and his wife taught me so much. In the primary relationships that these special people had, getting old or losing hair or being sick seemingly made little difference. They were always there for each

other. Always. They had family, a sense of duty, and a primitive faith in Something larger. That's what shines through now. He and Sharon had suffered the ravages of kidney disease. He lost his vigor, but never his caring heart and his need to do things the right way. I suspect that with all the changes, and through all the suffering, they relentlessly encouraged each other. There were very few harsh words, only support. They let each other know in the most intimate terms: "I'll be there, whatever you need, whatever you look like. I will be there." I know that's what the best relationships have at the core. Love bears all things.

So, driving back home, I think about those good people. Buddy, born less than fifty miles from where he was laid to rest, lived a good life. In the end, he was born, he fell in love, he did his best at everything, he held on for as long as he could, he trusted a faith, and he went out on his own terms. That seems good however you measure it. But, it rattles something deep in me and I don't yet know what it is. I suspect it's something with transitions and death and life and faith and relationships. I just suspect that.

Weeks later, my sleep is restless, and the depression seems episodic. I am at the beginning of the birth of Sheila. Somehow, I feel deep within my bones a belief that "this too shall pass". In the meantime, I hope Buddy is walking those streets of gold his preacher talked about. I hope he can smoke like a chimney, drink Cokes, Red Nehi, and cold water until he can't move. That's what I hope.

Thirty years have passed since that afternoon that the head dialysis nurse came in unannounced to my office. I was brand new. I had a little window that looked out on the parking lot. I was watching the patients as they left after a four-hour treatment. Some stumbled, some vomited. Some, too tired to even walk, were wheeled to waiting cars by family. My nurse was mad at me, and I didn't understand why she made such a big deal out of my looking outside. "Doc, only two rules you got to live by. Two. One, never, ever, ever watch the parking lot at shift change. It will break your heart. Two, never go to funerals of your patients." I think I now understand.

The Meaning of Christmas

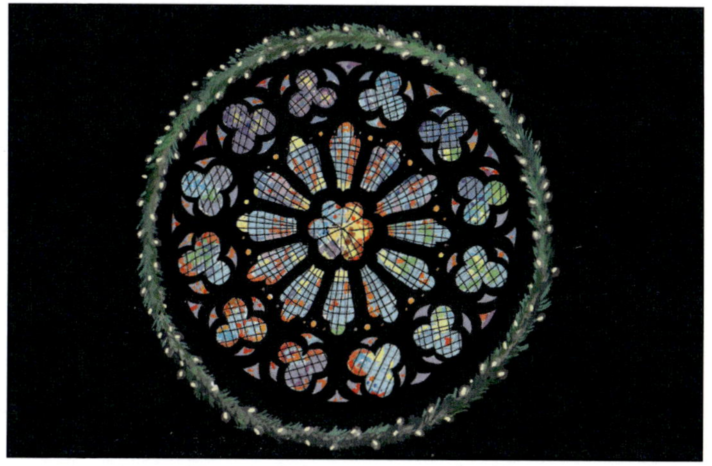

"The path of awakening is not about becoming who your are.
Rather it is about unbecoming who you are not."

—ALBERT SCHWEITZER

I t is Christmas, 2017. Alone for the first time in many
years, I am doing a retreat of sorts at a lovely inn just
north of Santa Fe. It is the heart of Georgia O'Keeffe

country. In an ancient valley, the land is firm, and people are kind. I need that just now. There is a kinetic energy here. I don't know if it is the beautiful flat-topped mountain that bursts out of the scruffy high-desert flats above Abiquiu or the chiseled canyons that boundary the snaking stream bed in the verdant valley ravine. Whatever, the landscape is erotic. There is a deep pulling to lay down on the flat dirt, suck in a relentless howling wind, and make love to the muses that haunt the deep canyons. The terrain is alien in its magnificent way. The distance and forever unfolding vistas are not boundary; they are simply reminder. In such a foreign place, the spirit is lifted to something different, if not higher. Artists for a century have come to find the rhythm and the resonance that is present. The ancient valley stands immutable but astonishingly alive.

It is five months since I have moved into a new place. In a past life I am Dad, doctor, mister. I am certain and solid. I honor the Hippocratic Oath and do my best day after day for scores of years. But, festering far in the depths of my being is another form. It is a feminine energy that I episodically feel at deep levels. It is the fuel that knows medicine as art, the muse that urges my artistic stabs of writing constantly in a small journal, it is the sentiment that loves poetry and orders roses for others. It is sweet and nurturing, but distant. But late in this journey, it cries to be honored. I am doing the best I can.

I drive to Santa Fe late on Christmas Eve. I have on

my warm Stuart Weitzman cadet grey boots and a snug fitting twill dress. The plaza is ablaze with drama and lights. Couples walk hand in hand. I stand in the cold before the beauty of the St. Francis church. There is a giant lighted wreath towering above us. It is round and complete and resonant. The doors open and I shuttle in. I have never found great comfort in the Christian narratives, but the massive Christ figure that looms over the sanctuary is vibrant this night. The rhythm of the old hymns and familiar words of the Birth feel solid and clean. The other-worldly Handel and Rutter music frame a force that is palpable. Whatever the legend, I am reminded that I am human and owe a death. But, I feel the visceral hope and sense the belief in an eternal Mystery forcing its way for millennia into the human story. The music, the litany, the spectacle, all offer a magnificent ritual. Driving back in the depth of night I have found comfort in things not seen.

I sit alone at a lovely Christmas brunch. The hotel, so well-tended, takes great pride in this meal. I have had reservations for weeks. Just as I start to eat, a blond, nice looking, middle-aged woman asks me to join her and her friend. The conversation is random but deeply felt. I say several times what I feel: deep gratitude for being asked to join. After they finish and leave, I sit in my space and know what it means to be alone in this world. It is at such times I am reminded how touching humans can be. There is a reality in the grace found within the kindness of strangers. Later, I walk around the large brown lake

formed by a dam. The sky is rich in a royal blue hue. Jet trails somehow form a cross as the sun reflects and settles. What a lovely day I have had.

I drive to Ojo Caliente the morning after Christmas. It is a place of ancient and healing waters that has been resurrected as spa and hotel. I persist in wearing rose colored fingernail polish. It is a badge of courage and honor. My massage therapist is Heidi. She is pretty in an earthy and solid way. She wears no makeup. She informs me she never has. We each share our narratives. I am struck by the fluid nature of her entire life. Fifty years old, she paints houses and does body work to pay bills. Her artistic talent unwinds with her ceramics. She has no significant other but has made a deep commitment to raise two dogs. She loves them dearly it seems. I ask her about her spiritual life. She is honest and has nothing that she can wrap her soul around, but finds comfort in the wisdom of a channeled Being. She aims to get more serious about meditation.

The gestalt in the room changes when I ask her what she has great passion about. She hesitates and says in a quiet but emphatic tone: "salsa". She goes on for a long time about the deep relationship that she has developed with this dance form. She describes the different styles, the nuances of the music, the type of men she partners with, and the various nationalities that come by it naturally. There is a wistfulness and a fullness in her voice when she talks about "being swept away". When I ask

her where she dances these days, she says, "I don't, but I will. I am raising my dogs just now."

Later, I climb one of the guardian peaks that surround the complex. I can see the fullness of the Rockies as they majestically process to the north. To the east is the edge of the Sangre de Cristo range hovering almost ominous in nearness. It rises like the back of a massive sleeping giant. I ponder in the silence and feel the buffering of a gently whispering wind. I am alive and awake. To be fully present in my own life is the sweetest feeling.

In this short journey, I have touched great mystery. I have felt the firm support of an ancient land, been lifted by the timeless resonance of a late-night ritual, been given hope by the sharing from another human, and been reminded that these bodies find what they need to love. I leave the valley lighter, having given birth to a new vision. It is One still wrapped in swaddling and crying to find what it loves to love, in the mystery that lies just ahead.

"I wish I could say I understand."

> *"All changes, even the most longed for, have their melancholy,
> for what we leave behind us is a part of ourselves; we must
> die to one life before we can enter into another."*
>
> —ANATOLE FRANCE

It is the first day of 2018. I am out of the closet. I have sent emails to a score of friends and classmates about my transgender status. If I had any idea about turning back, the bridge is burned. Among those I have notified is a former governor and a past CEO of a multinational company. So much for hiding out.

This is the response I get from a longtime friend and patient: "Well, Sheila, I wish I could say I didn't gasp when I read your letter. I wish I could say I understand but I don't. Not yet anyway. But I do know that God does

not make junk and that He loves us no matter what. So I will delight in remaining friends with you. Who can't use another girlfriend? But if I know you, you have visited every possible angle. For me, the most important aspect is that you know that I know nothing about what you are going through and have gone through. Yet, my respect and love for you is unchanged. I wish you a fabulous journey, and success wherever it takes you. I will miss my male friend but look forward to getting to know you and the woman you have become." I have known her for over twenty years. I was her aging mother's doctor, and her husband's physician as well. Her elegant response is so natural and honest. I cry deeply.

This is the response I get from a CEO, a man I have known for over thirty years: "Sheila, thanks for sending me this note. I know I will never fully appreciate what tensions you have experienced throughout life. I hope and pray you get the support now for this journey." He means what he says.

These are good and solid people. They live lives with meaning, with intent, with devotion. Their response is perhaps the best that I can hope for in that they are willing to listen to what I have to say. They are willing to learn. In the best of worlds, I am seen as a teacher with a modern message; in the worst, I am an old, retired doctor, gone deep over the edge.

I feel really alone at this point. I am far from home, and it seems there are dark and brooding clouds on

the horizon. How can my life have come to this? Such a random journey, it must seem. I wish I could talk to my Dad just now. He would know what to say, what to do. He always did. What would he say about all of this? I suspect he would be thoughtful and smile, and say, "Do your best. But if you are going to do it, be the best damn dressed woman in the world!" I think of Frodo and Sam in Tolkien's beautiful *The Lord of the Rings* trilogy. Deep in Mordor on a desperate path and doomed to a likely death, they hang on when all seems lost. Do I have that sort of courage and resolve? We shall see. But, one thing is for certain: I am far down a singular path that has no pat answers. Everything is new and full of danger; dread can blind me in the most sudden and offensive ways.

I think just now of my paternal grandfather. Beloved Pop. John Oliver was a handsome man who loved his family and life. He worked like a demon and could seemingly do anything. At times he was a butcher, an electrician, a carpenter, a grocer man, a roustabout. He had this beautiful silver hair and a widow's peak that made him look like he stepped off a Hollywood set. But, he was so gentle with me. He answered all the questions a precocious child could muster. He was there cheering as I, with blush on my cheeks and ruby lipstick on my lips, sang with abandon on stage, "I'm my Daddy's pride and joy." Perhaps he sensed some deep part of me yet unexplored. Every Tuesday he would pick me up in the late model blue and white Packard he was so proud of. We would drive north

on a narrow road to a small farm he had. There he would let me steer the tractor while I sat in his lap, or hunt giant bullfrogs with the bow and arrow that he bought me. Pop loved that little boy but accepted that this little soul loved to make jewelry and to play the piano. We would talk, and he would light his Viceroys one after another, and give thought to whatever I said. The smoke curled around him. It made him seem more earthy and human in an odd way. He always seemed so grounded and comfortable in all that he did. I loved him deeply. One summer day he coughed up blood. It was only two months until he lay dying on a lumpy hospital bed, which was five blocks from his beloved grocery store and less than a mile from his home on 18th Street. I lived close-by in a little brown and brick house. I would walk to the hospital most days, and I remember asking him for a dollar for something I had my heart set on at "Toyland". My mother was agitated that I would even think of such a thing at that desperate time. Pop grabbed his wallet and smiled that bright smile. He gave me his last dollar. He always seemed to do the next right thing.

The reason I think of Pop just now is because I remember the day he died. It was a Saturday morning in September, and I was about to eat warm chocolate donuts and drink cold Gandy's milk while I watched "Howdy Doody". As I walk past my parent's bedroom in our small space, my father sits propped up against the sand colored backboard. He says, "Gig, I need to tell you

something." He pauses and slowly shakes his head like he cannot believe he has to say this: "Pop is gone. He won't be coming back."

You must understand, my father gave up the study of architecture, which he dearly loved, to learn business so he could return and help my grandfather in his grocery store. Pop was my father's mentor and confidante; they were inseparable. In the truest sense: soulmates. Tonight, though, sitting here in a condo, far away from home, I know, finally, what my father must have felt on that early autumn day when he had lost his hero. He was alone for the first time in a dangerous world.

There are no firm answers in this process. It makes me weep, but how strange: now I hang more deeply on the smallest kindness and any splinter of compassion. Somehow, gentleness is more accessible. For all this that has come to my door, I am becoming softer it seems. In this dark night, I realize for the first time that I am just at the very beginning of a long journey learning what it means to be a woman.

Room 389

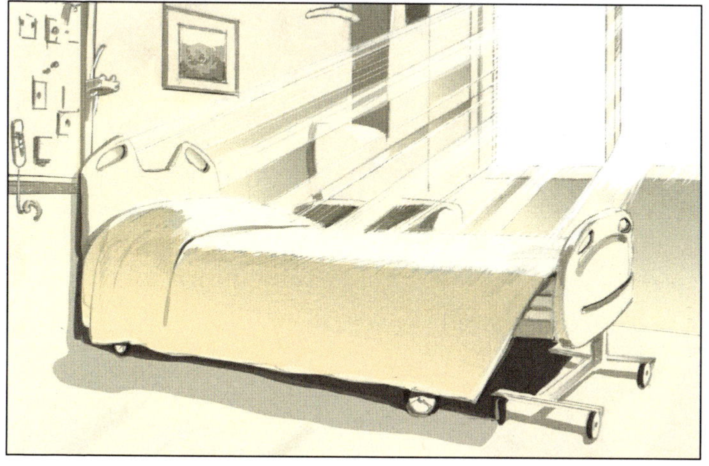

"Someday, the light will shine like a sun through my skin and they will say, 'What have you done with your life?' And though there are many moments I will remember, in the end, I will be proud to say, 'I was one of us.'"

—BRIAN ANDREAS

During my practice years, I was shepherd to people through the trajectory of the mystery that is critical care and trauma. I was at the side of

others as they addressed chronic illness and learned how to negotiate the drama the body can so forcefully create. However, when I consider it all, I treasure most the honor of being a guide at the end of life.

In the hospital, we had a special room where people who had decided to stop dialysis went to die. Room 389 was a room of comfort. It sat at the end of a long hallway with carpet that was an earthy brown color. It was a big room, with large chairs and enough direct sun to flood the space on summer days. It was just next to the elevators, so people could come and go as they wished. When no one was actively dying, it was just another patient room. But, during the many years I worked on that floor, that space always had a special feel to it. And meaning.

We do not do death well in our culture. Like gender, it is taboo. It is simply a fact constellated at birth that is chronically assumed but never discussed. Death and dying have become valuable commodities. The funeral home industry is Leviathan. It sells to "big media" a prevarication that sanitizes and distances us from experiencing the end of life as a sacred part of our journey. Now, we look to hospitals and funeral homes to negotiate that shadowy land for us. No one dies at home. In our constricted culture, that is considered wrong, almost criminal.

In the early part of the century, people died in their own bed. They were laid to rest in simple graves on their own land. Death was not adversarial; it was transformational. Not an enemy to be fought at each turn, but a

consort to guide us step by step. Now, everyone dies in the hospital; if not in a room, in the Emergency Room. We are taken to the morgue and then whisked away to be buried or cremated in rote rituals that typically cost thousands and thousands of dollars. Death has become a shadow-show produced by greed and directed by ignorance. It is not only the public that falls prey to this complex; physicians are culpable as well. We ignore the desperate need to educate the patient and family about the process of death, to discuss the options, and to be fully available at all times once the end of life ritual begins in earnest.

I did not always have such a vision. In my struggle with addiction, I had to wake up. Forced to grapple with my own mortality, I knew it was important to help others negotiate this part of life. Help and guidance were desperately needed, yet rarely offered. In my work, it was a constant. People died frequently. How odd, for years I avoided talk of the fear and anxiety that swirled like a tornado around me and my fatally ill patients. While in treatment, I was forced to deal with my own inevitable death and that made it easier to begin to dialogue with others. Denial of all things human is always the first hurdle. Once I made this choice, to be an advocate in this dark realm, I began to learn that there is a process that is "end of life". It has rules and implications that must be honored. How does the body change at the end of the process? How does one facilitate the transition to making it easier to "cross over"? How do I involve families so that all feel included?

How do we honor the death? What rituals can be involved to concretize the power and authority that are the roof beams in the archetypal house of our ending?

Room 389 was an anomaly. It was an island in a sea of despair where life was celebrated as it came to a close. Once a person made the decision to enter that room they became different. It was not only loved ones who sensed the change, but staff could feel it as well. It was a time at the end of the journey when all pretense could drop. There was nothing left to hide. This was the end of a long migration from birth to death, and, in deference, these people were seen for what they were: something special and apart.

Settling into room 389 was the first step into a new realm, but it was a precious step and one that certainly set the tone for the transition ahead. There, people came to pay respects, to express thanks, to recall joy at a life well lived, or to honor a long friendship. It was a way station for those in process, be they mother, father, husband, wife, or child. It attracted attentive nurses and caring chaplains who marshaled and infused positive energy and intent. With the myriad good words that were passed in final tribute, it had a metaphysical sparkle and unearthly glow. It was a good place to die. I am proud of the work we did there.

As I think of that time, I am looking at a picture taken from my favorite chair in the upstairs of my home. It looks out on a beautiful vista of sky and water. When I looked

far down the road before I left the confines of that soft chair to honor my transgender transformation, I knew that there would be times when I would look back and be sad. I could not have prepared for such a rush of overwhelming grief. The tears pour out. The sadness simmers like the lingering residue from the wakes we would have when a patient, now comatose on the bed in 389, was nearing an end.

I remember my maternal grandfather, a stoic and honest man. He was short, squat, and chewed constantly on a cigar. His shirts all had tobacco juice stains. It fit him so well. He was so genuine in a gentle sort of way. A self-made man, he worked tirelessly from the day at age five that his mother answered a knock at their door. Her husband, the postmaster in a Central Texas town, had inexplicably been run over by a train. Somehow his car, perched on the tracks at mid-day, had not moved as the locomotive barreled down.

As he grew older, I would, when I could, go to eat lunch with my grandfather. In our usual table at our favorite Mexican food restaurant, I was quick to wolf down the green enchiladas. He would make short work of three crispy tacos. Our talk was always random. One day, for some odd reason, I asked him what he would miss most when he died. He smiled an ironic smile, stuck the cigar back into its constant position and said: "I'm just going to miss seeing how everything turns out with all those people I love."

Strangely, there is a coherent resonance in the rambling remembrances about end of life care, a favorite old chair, and a grandfather's lament. Bidden or unbidden, these are events that decorate my journey. They are precious and special processes that define a life now in flux.

You see, the doctor, the mister, the man, is dying. He has entered 389. At an ending, as days run on, he waits patiently to be swallowed by the sacred feminine. He thinks of so many good things and hopes that whatever it is that is destined on the other side, she will get to see how everything has turned out with all those people she has loved.

CPSIA information can be obtained
at www.ICGtesting.com
Printed in the USA
BVHW081350081121
621068BV00005B/185

9 781991 217639